THE WIZARD

THE WIZARD
sorcery through the ages

ALAN BAKER

EBURY
PRESS

To Ana, Geni, Maria,
and Rafa, for magical days

First published in Great Britain in 2003

1 3 5 7 9 10 8 6 4 2

Ebury Press
Random House, 20 Vauxhall Bridge Road, London SW1V 2SA

Random House Australia (Pty) Limited
20 Alfred Street, Milsons Point, Sydney, New South Wales 2061, Australia

Random House New Zealand Limited
18 Poland Road, Glenfield, Auckland 10, New Zealand

Random House South Africa (Pty) Limited
Endulini, 5A Jubilee Road, Parktown 2193, South Africa

The Random House Group Limited Reg. No. 954009

www.randomhouse.co.uk

A CIP catalogue record for this book is available from the British Library

ISBN 009188912X

Typeset by seagulls
Cover Design by the Senate

Printed and bound in Great Britain by Mackays of Chatham plc

Papers used by Ebury Press are natural, recyclable products
made from wood grown in sustainable forests

Grateful acknowledgement is given
for permission to quote from the following:
An Encyclopedia of Occultism by Lewis Spence, Citadel Press, New York.
The Magical Arts by Richard Cavendish, A. P. Wayy Ltd., London.

CONTENTS

'Scripture rightly prohibits the use of magic, but the associates of magicians are apostate and evil spirits and foul demons. For no good spirit obeys a magician.'

ORIGEN, *HOMILIES*

'... happy is the tomb where no wizard hath lain, and happy the town at night whose wizards are all ashes.'

H. P. LOVECRAFT, 'THE FESTIVAL'

INTRODUCTION

The Serpent's Promise

'God doth know that in the day ye eat thereof, then your eyes shall be opened and ye shall be as gods, knowing good and evil.'

Thus the serpent in the Garden of Eden persuades Adam and Eve to eat the fruit of the Tree of Knowledge. Traditionally, of course, the snake is a symbol of evil, but to the wizard it represents wisdom and he therefore seeks knowledge, so that this promise to the first humans is at last fulfilled. Behind the wizard's myriad rituals and incantations, his signs and sigils, his dark tomes and obscure treatises, lies a single ambition: to make himself a god.

The wizard is alive and well in the twenty-first century. Even in our sophisticated and cynical age, his ability to enchant is undiminished, and we continue to wonder at his dark and awesome powers, even as our intellectual élite offers us exasperated reminders that such powers cannot and never could exist. Recently, he has reappeared in popular culture in the guise of the young trainee wizard Harry Potter, who has captured the imaginations of children and adults all over the world, and who stands with one foot in the drab world of the mundane and the other in the archetypal realms of magic. Looming behind the diminutive, bespectacled Harry stands the majestic figure of the wizard Gandalf, who is also working his magic on cinema screens across the globe in the ambitious three-part adaptation of J.R.R. Tolkien's classic fantasy *The Lord of the Rings*, guaranteeing the original book a new generation of devoted readers. These characters are familiar to millions, and yet behind them, and all the other heroes and villains of literature and film who have used magic in the pursuit of good or evil, stands their true inspiration – a figure cloaked in the perilous darkness of the arcane and esoteric, that reaches through the centuries to proclaim the awesome power of the supernatural. This is the real wizard, a practitioner of magic who has appeared in many guises throughout history.

While the image of Harry Potter attending a school for wizards is, of course, quite charming, and guaranteed to galvanise the imaginations of the young, it has many dark antecedents in the history of witchcraft and demonology.

Demonology can be defined as that branch of magic that deals with malevolent spirits, supernatural beings that are not deities as such. This occult science was practised in the Middle Ages by Jews and Christians, who maintained philosophical communications with the Moors of Spain. At that time, Spain had three great schools of magic at Toledo, Seville and Salamanca. In the latter city, demonology was taught in a vast, dark cavern in order to emphasise the seriousness and solemnity of the subject, and the tutors in magic taught that knowledge and power could be obtained with the assistance of fallen angels. This is a subject we will examine in greater detail later in this book.

The wizard is part of the collective consciousness of humanity. Through the centuries, the magical workings he performed in reality were as rivers feeding the great ocean of the human imagination and we have always regarded with awe those among us who possess (or claim to possess) the ability to influence in profound ways the world around us.

One of the most famous magicians in the Western literary tradition is, of course, Faust, the great wizard and necromancer who sold his soul to Satan in return for youth, knowledge and occult power. The Faust figure of legend and literature has become a potent symbol for the danger inherent in human arrogance and hubris. However, he was much more than an invention of myth: there is sound evidence that such a person existed.

Johann Faust was a brilliant magician who flourished in the sixteenth century. He travelled widely throughout Europe, performed many magical feats, and died in mysterious circumstances.

The wizard Trithemius mentions him in a letter written in 1507, writing in less than flattering terms of his foolishness and arrogance, while Mudt, a canon of the German Church, also writes of him as a charlatan. However, Johann Gast, a Protestant pastor of Basel, seems to have known Faust personally, and believed that a horse and dog belonging to him were in fact familiar spirits. The demonologist Wier described him as a drunkard who had studied magic at Cracow, and that he met his death by strangulation at the hands of Satan himself.

What seems clear enough is that Faust was a wandering wizard and necromancer who gained quite a reputation for himself. By the end of the sixteenth century, he had become the very model of the medieval wizard, and countless folk tales and stories were attached to his name. The first printed version of his life is the *Volksbuch* (1587) of Johann Spiess, a work that, when translated into English, served as the inspiration for Christopher Marlowe's play *Dr Faustus*. These works picture Faust as a man of irredeemable evil, who suffers eternal damnation for his transgressions against God, for 'the wickedness of believing in the all-sufficiency of human knowledge', in the words of the occult historian Lewis Spence.

Other writers saw Faust as the symbol of a heroic (as opposed to evil) striving for knowledge and power, and therefore as worthy of salvation. The ultimate pinnacle of this viewpoint is, of course, Goethe's *Faust*, one of the greatest dramatic poems ever written. Goethe expanded upon the original legend, adding the elements of redemptive love and the saving power of the feminine principle. His masterwork inspired, in turn, many other tellings of the Faust story, most notably in the twentieth century by Thomas Mann, whose novel *Doktor Faustus* appeared in 1947. In addition, it inspired many composers of operas, oratorios and symphonies, including Berlioz, Gounod, Schumann and Liszt.

The idea of the Faustian pact with dark forces that possess the ability to rain physical and spiritual destruction upon those foolish enough to have dealings with them has ancient origins. As Spence notes in his *Encyclopaedia of Occultism*: 'The idea of the pact with Satan belongs to both Jewish and Christian magico-religious belief, but is probably more truly Kabbalistic than anything else, and can scarcely be traced further back.'

The Faust legend extends through the tradition of Western magic. It is a measure of its potency that the Faust idea finds a modern expression in the mistrust felt by many people towards scientific advances (for example, nuclear power and genetic engineering) that are perceived to have extended beyond the boundaries of humanity's moral and ethical capacity.

However, it is from Merlin and Gandalf that we take the classic image of the wizard as the tall, gaunt, robed figure (frequently in a pointed hat) wandering across dark and wild landscapes, chanting spells and incantations beneath violent, cloud-strewn skies. There is some truth in this image, particularly with regard to the places in which magical workings were judged most likely to succeed. According to *The Key of Solomon,* one of the most powerful and dangerous of magical grimoires, the best places to perform magical rituals were desolate regions far from the dwelling places of other humans. The shores of lakes, forests, abandoned houses, mountains, caves and crossroads were considered most suitable.

The grimoires were books of ceremonial magic giving instructions on how to summon evil spirits, destroy one's enemies, force women to submit in love, and so on. However, these books, which contain instructions on enlisting supernatural aid in committing the most heinous of crimes, are also filled with prayers to God and His angels. According to the historian of occultism Richard Cavendish, in his book *The Magical Arts:*

> The principal process in the *Grimoire of Honorius,* which is usually considered the most diabolical of them all, overflows with impassioned and perfectly sincere appeals to God and devout sayings of Mass. It also involves tearing out the eyes of a black cock and slaughtering a lamb, and its purpose is to summon up the Devil.

However, the wizard has had many faces, and many methods of manifesting in the popular psyche. There was, for example, the dashing scoundrel Count Alessandro Cagliostro, who was born in Italy in 1745, and whose acquaintance we shall be making in greater detail later. After committing various crimes in Sicily, Cagliostro fled from the island and travelled throughout Europe, practising sorcery and alchemy with his wife, Lorenza Feliciani. He was welcomed in the homes of the most distinguished families on the Continent, and by the sale of love philtres, magic elixirs and other strange potions, he amassed considerable wealth. His shady character ensured his involvement in numerous scandals, which forced him to move regularly from one country to another. The legendary reputation he acquired included that of a successful necromancer, and the ability to fashion diamonds by alchemical means.

It is not always appreciated that the wizard was active during classical antiquity; the literature of the period provides many examples of the escapades of sorcerers. No less a figure than Pliny the Elder described magic in his voluminous *Natural History* as 'a thing detestable in itself', adding that although 'frivolous and false' it nevertheless contained 'some element of truth'. There were also many figures of the period with whom we would not normally associate the practice of magic, and yet who researched the subject with the greatest enthusiasm. According to Pliny, the Emperor Nero was 'inclined to study the Magical art as assiduously as to play upon the cythera and to hear and sing tragic songs'. Such was the enormity of his wealth and the corruption of his mind that he possessed a 'desire to command the gods and familiar spirits'. Unfortunately for Nero, it was said that the spirits who might have given him the supernatural power he sought would not appear to or aid people who had freckles or pimples – and Nero had an abundance of both. This did not deter him, however, and he enlisted the aid of Tyridates, King of Armenia, as teacher. Tyridates, a great magician, travelled to Rome by land because he considered it unlawful to spit or otherwise discharge bodily fluids into the sea, 'which might pollute and defile that Element'. In spite of his tutoring, it seems that Nero 'could never receive at his hands the skill of this Science'.

We can see from these few examples that our traditional image of the wizard is far from complete. He exists in all times and places, beginning perhaps with the post-Deluge Zoroastrian wizards, and continuing with the Neolithic shaman, the medieval sorcerer, the Renaissance alchemist and mystic, the eighteenth-century rake, and the modern occultist of the twentieth century. It is as a result of his physical and temporal ubiquity that he has proved so profoundly influential in the cultural life of humanity.

From the earliest days of human civilisation, there have been those who were believed to have the ability to control the hidden forces of the supernatural. Despite the fact that scientific materialism has triumphed over occultism and superstition, our fascination with witchcraft, black magic, astrology and many other aspects of this world continues unabated. There are several reasons for this, not least of which is our hunger for mystery, for that which cannot be explained by the sterile formulae of a glib and arrogant scientific establishment. Indeed, the word 'occult' means 'that which is hidden', and it is the hidden, the unknown, that has always fascinated us. In addition, the practitioners of the magical arts, be they wizards, witches, shamans, necromancers or alchemists, represent a very powerful cultural icon, unrestrained by national or ethnic boundaries. The principles of magic are universal principles that have been studied throughout history and all over the world. Such icons retain their power to mystify and fascinate even in the present day, in the face of scientific rationalism and scepticism. Indeed, there is a powerful case for claiming that sorcery was itself the precursor of science, and as such holds an important position in the history of human thought.

To the modern rationalist, the principles of magic to which the wizard adheres are nothing more than superstition and mumbo-jumbo – naïve at best, idiotic and dangerous at worst. But the occult sciences are not random: they have very clearly defined laws and logic, although it is a logic that would mean much more to an artist or poet than to a mathematician or physical scientist. As Cavendish states in *The Magical Arts*, magical logic

> leaps to conclusions which are usually scientifically unwarranted, but which often seem poetically right. It is a type of thinking which has been prevalent all through the history of Europe, which lies behind huge areas of our religion, philosophy and literature, and which is a major guide-post to the regions of the supernatural, the regions of which science has nothing to say.

It would be a mistake to see the wizard as an irrelevance today, as a relic of a remote and much simpler time. Occultism in most of its forms is of considerable interest to the public throughout the world; indeed, it has attracted more interest in the last century than at any time since the Renaissance – a fact that is frequently bemoaned by the scientific community. In Italy, for instance, there are many groups practising black magic, especially in rural communities, and ritual exorcism is frequently employed, sometimes with the wholehearted approval of professional psychiatrists. In 1985, there were just twenty Church-appointed exorcists in Italy; today, there are three hundred.

The most famous exorcist in Italy is undoubtedly Father Gabriele Amorth, who, at the age of seventy-seven, has been a priest for fifty years and is the leader of Rome's six exorcists, as well as President of the International Association of Exorcists.

Father Amorth, who fought with the Italian Resistance during the Second World War and studied law before entering the Church, maintains that there are many grades of demonic possession, and that sufferers often try to conceal it. This is a far cry from the popular idea of the possessed person, such as the young girl, Regan, so memorably portrayed by Linda Blair in William Friedkin's 1973 film *The Exorcist*. It seems that demonic possession does not always involve projectile-vomiting pea soup and turning one's head 360 degrees. According to Amorth, the

Devil prefers to work his evil without people knowing who is at the bottom of it, although there are some cases where the possession causes such intense physical pain to the victim that it becomes obvious (to believers) who is responsible.

Although belief in possession by evil spirits is widespread in Italy, particularly in rural areas, it is essential not to confuse it with ordinary illness, and Amorth advises people to consult doctors before turning to exorcists. The symptoms of possession can include headaches and cramps, which, of course, may well have a non-supernatural cause. The priest also recognises that what may look like possession can usually be explained as epilepsy, schizophrenia or other mental maladies. He estimates that of the thousands of people who have gone to him for help, only about a hundred or so have been genuinely possessed by demonic forces.

An exorcist can tell if a person is possessed by their violent aversion to all things holy, such as the Sacrament. Showing them the crucifix will subdue them immediately and examining the person's eyes at various times during the exorcism ritual by gently lifting the eyelids shows whether they are truly possessed, as their eyes roll up or down to such an extent that their pupils are very hard to discern. During the ritual, the exorcist requires the assistance of another priest, and a group of lay people to help with the saying of prayers. He begins with the words 'Behold the Cross of the Lord' and touches the victim's neck with the hem of his stole. Holy water and salt are very effective at getting the demons to show themselves (holy water for obvious reasons, and salt because it is a preservative, a means to prevent decay and putrefaction, which evil spirits are very fond of).

Demons do not like to talk to the exorcist, and yet the exorcist must interrogate them carefully. The demon speaks through the victim, in an unnatural voice. He may be Satan himself, or another demon; he may be alone or accompanied by many others in the victim's body. The exorcist must ascertain how it came to enter the victim, whether it was as the result of a black magic spell, and if so, the nature of that spell.

Once the battle has commenced, the demon will often display incredible strength: an exorcist will occasionally have to enlist the aid of several strong men to hold down even a small child while the ritual is conducted. Sometimes a patient will spit at the priest and vomit, while the demon threatens his enemy with all manner of calamities, eating the priest's heart, for instance, or putting hellish serpents in his bed. The one thing the exorcist must not display is fear; and indeed, there is little reason to feel fear, since the exorcist is protected by the power of God.

Father Amorth maintains that every demon has a weak spot, which the exorcist must find and attack. Some demons, for example, find it intolerable to have the Sign of the Cross traced on any part of the victim's body, while others will be severely weakened by the sprinkling of holy water. It is always possible to rid a person of his or her demons, but it is not always a swift process, and successful exorcisms may take weeks, months or even years to complete, with the victim returning to the priest at regular intervals.

A successful exorcism is a catastrophic defeat for the invading demon: once he is banished back to Hell, he can never again return to Earth to torment the souls of the living. As to the reasons for demonic possession, it may be the result of a person's dabbling in the occult, or it may be the result of a curse performed by an evil wizard or witch. No one is certain why more women than men become victims of possession. Representatives of the Catholic Church speculate that it may be because interest in the occult and paranormal tends to be more prevalent among women than men (it is difficult to say how true this is), or because Satan is using women to torment men, just as the Devil caused Adam's downfall through Eve.

As the Catholic Church struggles to modernise, there seems to be less of a place for exorcism than in previous years. Father Amorth bemoans the fact that the Catholic establishment now speaks more of the spirit of evil than of evil entities performing their foul deeds on Earth. The exorcists of today find themselves in a difficult position, with the Church telling them that they must first be absolutely certain that a demon is present in a patient before beginning the ritual. According to Amorth, this makes no sense, since it is only once an exorcism has begun that the demon can be made to reveal himself, and an exorcism performed on one who is not possessed, according to Amorth, causes no harm to that person.

Across the Atlantic and away from exorcism, Americans spend fortunes on power crystals and other occult paraphernalia to improve every aspect of their lives, and even consult psychics who claim the ability to communicate with their dead pets. All this in spite of the warnings from both sceptics and the mainstream religions that to meddle with the occult is a very bad idea; the former pointing out that to do so is to succumb to primitive, dark age thinking, and the latter warning of the dangers of opening oneself to powerful and malign forces.

However, to the occultist, the forces he or she attempts to utilise are not to be considered 'good' or 'evil' in themselves. Contrary to popular belief, no 'black magician' sees himself as such, not even Aleister Crowley, who earned the epithet 'the wickedest man in the world' from an outraged press on account of the sex and blood that figured prominently in his rituals. He considered himself an inhabitant of an altogether higher moral and intellectual plane than the black magicians he professed to despise, and among whom he included Christian Scientists and Spiritualists, as well as those fellow occultists who disapproved of his methods.

The wizard who performs what others would call black magic does not consider himself evil: he is above and beyond such petty distinctions. In order to control the Universe, which is his ultimate aim, he must strive for understanding and control of everything the Universe contains – evil and good, hatred and love, cruelty and kindness. The man who would gain mastery over the Universe must gain mastery over all things.

ONE

The Archetype

'The evil angels had sown the seeds of that strange art
among men and had introduced every kind of sorcery and
magic among them.'

EUSEBIUS, *PRAEPARATIO EVANGELICA*

The ideas concerning wizards and magic that we frequently associate with the creations of great fantasists like Tolkien have defi-
nite historical forerunners. The wizard Gandalf (and, of course,
his arch-rival Saruman) are obvious cases in point, as we have
said. Tolkien, in his capacity as mythmaker, drew heavily on
Norse and Celtic legends to realise his vision of Middle Earth,
and at the centre of the mythology of Britain (which, at least in
part, gave birth to Gandalf) stands Merlin, the wizard, seer and
teacher at the court of King Vortigern and later at the court of
King Arthur.

In Celtic folklore, Merlin was a bard and hero, and in
Arthurian legend he became famous as a wizard of immense
power and wisdom, and counsellor to the King. Formerly, it was
thought that the Arthurian legend was simply the work of various poets of the Middle Ages; however, the consensus now is
that the legend developed out of the stories of Celtic mythology,
the oldest of which appear in the Welsh *Mabinogion*. The wizard
Merlin occupies a pivotal position in the cultural history of
Britain, and indeed much of Europe. By the year 1000, the
legend had been transmitted from the Celts of North Britain to

the wandering minstrels of Brittany, who followed Norman armies across the western regions of the Continent. He stands as a link between our distant and mysterious pagan past and the Christian religion that supplanted it.

When the word 'wizard' is mentioned, Merlin is the name that immediately springs to mind. It is Merlin who reaches out to us from the dim and misty landscape of historical legend, who stands at the centre of the mythical landscape of magic and occult science. He is a primal force, representing a time now lost to us, when the lands of earth were steeped in the supernatural, and myths and monsters influenced human lives much more profoundly than they do today. He is an archetypal figure, whose shape-changing shadow falls heavily across all the sorcerers and workers of magic who came after him.

Merlin's mother, it is said, was seduced by a demon who took the form of a handsome youth, and who then vanished into thin air. When Merlin was born, his mother, fearing for his soul, immediately plunged him into a font of holy water. The water had the effect of instilling in him a love of humanity; but it was not enough to banish all the elements of his infernal origin, which manifested in his ability to change shape, his mastery of the magical arts and his voracious sexual appetite.

The first mention of King Arthur and Merlin occurs in the *History of the Kings of Britain* (*Historia Regum Britanniae*) by Geoffrey of Monmouth (*c.* 1136). In his (less than reliable) account, we are told that a fifth-century king named Vortigern ordered an impregnable fort to be constructed on Mount Snowdon in Wales. Vortigern was a chieftain who had proclaimed himself king when the Romans left Britain to concentrate on the defence of Rome against the barbarian invasions. His reign was soon threatened by the Picts, a savage people from the north. Vortigern recruited Saxon mercenaries to battle the Picts, but lacked the funds to pay them. As a result, the Saxons turned their attention to Vortigern's lands.

Vortigern's mountain fort kept collapsing, and the king's soothsayers told him that the project could only succeed if the stones were sprinkled with the blood of a boy who had no father. The king immediately ordered his soldiers to search for such a boy, and eventually they came upon Merlin. He and his mother were taken to Vortigern, who listened to the strange tale of the boy's conception.

The soothsayers were pleased, and told the king that this youth would make an ideal sacrifice, since he really did have no human father. With admirable presence of mind, the lad informed his captors that the fort kept collapsing because they were building upon waterlogged ground, which was undermining the foundations. The king ordered his men to dig down into the earth, and sure enough they discovered a subterranean pool of water. Merlin added that if they drained this pool, they would discover the remains of two dragons. Vortigern ordered his men to comply, and the two dragons were promptly uncovered. Vortigern was mightily impressed, and agreed to spare the boy's life.

Thereafter, Merlin made a number of prophecies, including the downfall of Vortigern, which indeed came to pass when he was besieged and killed in his own fortress. The Britons, relentlessly forced west by the Saxons, were rallied by Ambrosius Aurelianus, a soldier who had served in the Roman army, and who led them to many victories against the Saxon invaders. Ambrosius was succeeded by his brother, Uther Pendragon and the most brilliant of his generals was a man named Artorius – Arthur. The young general was instrumental in bringing a halt to the Saxon invasion, but his successes were undermined by infighting amongst his allies.

According to legend, of course, Arthur was Uther Pendragon's son. When Uther became king, all the nobles in the land were invited to the coronation, including Duke Gorlois, the ruler of Cornwall. Upon seeing Gorlois' beautiful wife, Ygern, Uther fell helplessly in love and resolved to possess her. Realising this, Gorlois took her back to his castle at Tintagel, which was virtually impregnable, standing as it did upon an island connected to the land by a narrow bridge.

Uther knew that there was only one way in which he might find himself alone with Ygern. He ordered Merlin to give him the power to change shape, so that he could assume the appearance of Gorlois and thus gain entry to the castle. Although he warned Uther that this course of action would result, ultimately, in the destruction of his line, Merlin complied. Uther gained entry to Gorlois' castle with ease, and made love to Ygern. When Gorlois was killed in battle, Uther married Ygern, and reigned for another fifteen years until he was assassinated. His son, Arthur, conceived when Uther took the shape of his rival, then became king.

This is the kernel of the legend of Arthur and Merlin. The famous tales of the sword in the stone and the Knights of the Round Table were added by later writers, most notably Sir Thomas Malory, whose *Morte d'Arthur* was published in 1485.

According to some scholars, Merlin himself was based on a Welsh bard of the late sixth century named Myrddin. The British writer Colin Wilson reminds us that Geoffrey of Monmouth probably changed the wizard's name because of Myrddin's similarity to the French *merde*, meaning 'shit'. '[A] magician named Myrddin would have invited ridicule in an age when England was ruled by the French.'

According to the historian Norma Lorre Goodrich, Merlin was born in Wales. She suggests that 'Merlin' was not actually his name, but rather his title (a merlin being a species of hawk). She further maintains that Myrddin and Merlin were two different people, that Merlin was a bishop named Dubricius, who crowned Arthur, and Myrddin was a poet who went mad and took to living wild in forests, where he gradually attained supernatural powers.

It is this person on whom Geoffrey of Monmouth based his *Life of Merlin*, the follow-up to *History of the Kings of Britain*, which concerns a Welsh prophet who lost his sanity following a battle against a Scottish king.

According to Nicolai Tolstoy in his 1985 book *The Quest for Merlin*, the wizard was the last of the druids, the priests of ancient Celtic Britain, Ireland and Gaul, known to have existed as far back as the third century BC. They were a mysterious people, and such information about them that has survived comes to us mainly from the Irish sagas as well as Roman writings, especially those of Julius Caesar. It seems that their religion revolved around the worship of several nature gods, and that they were a highly ritualistic priestly caste who were charged with the education of the young. Although they seem to have been literate, their preferred method of teaching was oral, with the educational process lasting as long as twenty years. They believed in the immortality of the soul; however, they did not believe that the soul would be judged in the afterlife. Their ceremonies involved both animal and human sacrifices, and were conducted in sacred groves and near rivers and lakes. There were a number of female druids: Tacitus mentions a tribe called the Bructeri who were led by a prophetess.

As to the ultimate fate of Merlin, legend has it that it was his lustful nature that led to his downfall. He had been raised by a witch named Nimue, who fell in love with him when he reached adulthood. When he rejected her, she was utterly devastated, but resolved to have him nevertheless. She embarked upon a plan that was a combination of possession and revenge. Like Merlin, Nimue was capable of changing her shape to whatever form she desired. She changed her shape to that of a beautiful woman and presented herself to her victim. Merlin had no hesitation in seducing her. They made love, and at the crucial moment, when Merlin was defenceless and totally distracted by ecstasy, Nimue transformed herself into a sphere of amber, completely enclosing him. With the great wizard trapped helpless within her, she again transformed, this time into an oak tree. It is said that Nimue and Merlin are locked together still, eternally a part of one another.

Thus ends the strange story of Merlin, our archetypal wizard. As with King Arthur, the legend describes his withdrawal from the human world, but not his death. While Arthur lies with his warriors in a secret cavern until his country needs him again, Merlin sleeps within the imprisoning body of a great oak tree, waiting to be set free.

TWO

The Shaman

> 'With visible breath I am walking.
> A voice I am sending as I walk.
> In a sacred manner I am walking.
> With visible tracks I am walking.
> In a sacred manner I walk.'
>
> BLACK ELK, *BLACK ELK SPEAKS*

Although he does not conform to the traditional image of the wise or wicked wizard in flowing robes and pointed hat, the shaman was the first member of humanity to which the name could be applied. The shaman was (and is) active in generally small-scale societies, and was believed to be able to diagnose, cure, and sometimes cause illnesses because of his special relationship with the natural environment and the myriad spirits inhabiting it. Different forms of shamanism are found around the world, and their practitioners are also known as medicine men and witch doctors. Shamanism is based on the belief that the entire world is pervaded by spirits and other invisible supernatural forces that have the power to affect the lives of human beings.

Shamans are not organised within ritual or spiritual associations, as are priests. The process of becoming a shaman is not an easy one: the altered state of consciousness that is required is not accessible to all, and many shamans achieve it only at a moment of great trauma, for example due to severe injury or illness. At the point where death is almost upon him, the prospective shaman may make contact with the spirits of the natural world, and, if he is strong and fortunate enough to survive the experience and return to health, he will find that he has attained a highly privileged position among his people.

From then on, it is the responsibility of the shaman to maintain contact with the spirits of nature. On the eve of a hunt, for instance, the shaman must re-enter the altered state of consciousness in order to contact the relevant spirits and ask their permission and blessing, so that the hunt will be successful. Likewise, when a person falls ill, it will be left to the shaman to consult the spirits as to the best course of action to take in order to ensure the recovery of the patient.

Some societies distinguish shamans that cure from those that cause harm; others believe that all shamans have both curative and deadly powers. They are usually paid for their services, and generally enjoy great power and prestige in the community; but they may also be suspected of harming others, and may thus be feared. Most shamans are men, but there are societies in which women may also hold the position. In some communities, the male shaman denies his own sexual identity by assuming the dress and attributes of a woman; this practice is rare, but has been observed among the Chukchi people of Siberia.

Shamans performed (and still perform) a vitally important function within this culture, in which ongoing interaction with the subtle yet immensely powerful world of nature and its spiritual denizens is of great significance in everyday life. It would be a serious mistake to look with amusement or condescension upon a shaman asking the permission of spirits to hunt their animals. Interaction with the spiritual aspects of existence through the offices of people possessing certain 'qualifications' is as familiar a concept in our own culture as in those in North America or Siberia.

A particularly striking and moving example of the call to shamanism can be found in the life of the Oglala Sioux holy man Black Elk, who was born in 1863 at Little Powder River, and was the second cousin of Crazy Horse. The story of Black Elk's life, including how he became a shaman, is immortalised in the classic book *Black Elk Speaks*, which was published in 1932 by the Nebraska poet John G. Neihardt. The book is based on conversations Neihardt had with Black Elk while the former was researching a book on the history of the American West. Although the book's message made little impact during the Depression, in the following decades it enjoyed a steadily increasing readership among those seeking a more profound alternative to the cold and inhuman industrialism that ruled their lives and, indeed, their very consciousness.

In the growing spiritual awareness of the 1960s, *Black Elk Speaks* provided a focus for the increasing interest in the religious beliefs and practices of the Plains Indians. Aside from the peerless insight the book provides into these beliefs for non-Native Americans, it has also proved to be of enormous importance for new generations of young Native Americans who desire to re-establish contact with their traditions. As Vine Deloria Jr. writes:

> To them the book has become a North American Bible of all tribes. They look to it for spiritual guidance, for sociological identity, for political insight, and for affirmation of the continuing substance of Indian tribal life, now being badly eroded by the same electronic media, which are dissolving other American communities.

There is no typical path to shamanism, but Black Elk's story is an interesting one.

It was during the summer when he was five years old that Black Elk first heard the voices. He was playing alone when they came to him, and at first he thought it was his mother calling him, but when he turned to look, there was no one there. This happened on several occasions, and Black Elk began to grow frightened and ran home.

Not long afterwards he went out riding with a bow and arrows his grandfather had made for him. There was a thunderstorm developing to the west, and just as he entered some woods along a creek, he noticed a kingbird sitting on the limb of a tree. Placing an arrow in his bow, Black Elk took aim at the bird and was about to shoot, when the bird spoke to him. It said, 'The clouds all over are one-sided.'

The boy had no idea what this meant, although Black Elk told John Neihardt that it may have meant that the clouds were watching him. The bird then said, 'Listen! A voice is calling you.'

The boy then looked up at the clouds, and saw two men riding down from the sky towards him, 'head first, like arrows slanting down'. They came from the north, and sang a sacred song telling him that a sacred voice was calling him, accompanied by the titanic drumming of the thunder from the west.

Black Elk sat upon his horse in amazement, watching the approach of the figures. When they were almost upon him, they wheeled about and were transformed into geese. And then they were gone, and there was nothing but the rain and the wind and the thunder. For some time, he kept the vision to himself. 'I liked to think about it,' he said, 'but I was afraid to tell it.'

For the next four years, life went on as normal. Occasionally, when he was out alone, Black Elk would hear the voices again, calling to him, although he did not understand what they wanted him to do. This did not happen very often, however, and when the voices were silent he forgot about them and the strange vision he had experienced.

When he was nine years old, he heard a voice again. It was summer, and the Oglala Sioux were moving towards the Rocky Mountains. One evening they were camped in a valley beside a small creek and while he was eating, Black Elk heard the words, 'It is time; now they are calling you.'

'The voice was so loud and clear,' he said, 'that I believed it, and I thought I would just go where it wanted me to go.' Without a word, he set his meal aside, stood up and left the tepee. But when he stood outside, the voice was silent, and his thighs began to hurt. It was, he said, as if he had awoken from a dream, re-entering the mundane world where there were no visions and no voices from the sky.

The next day, Black Elk collapsed, and became weak and sick. He was carried to his parents' tepee, where his mother and father watched over him, deeply concerned. The entrance to the tepee was open, and through it Black Elk suddenly saw the two men he had seen in his earlier vision. As before, they were coming from the clouds, but each now carried a long spear, and from their points lightning flashed in jagged tendrils that lit up the air. This time, they did not transform themselves into geese, but came right down to the ground, and stood looking at him. Together, the riders from the sky exclaimed, 'Hurry! Come. Your Grandfathers are calling you.'

The men then flew away like arrows fired upwards from a bow, and Black Elk no longer felt sick and weak. He got up from his bed and left his parents' tepee. He could see a small cloud approaching very fast, hurtling across the sky towards him. When it reached him, the cloud came down to the ground and enveloped him, taking him up into the sky and carrying him away in the direction from which it had come. Black Elk looked down, and could see his mother and father standing beside their tepee.

This experience is common in those who are about to become shamans, and bears a striking resemblance to the so-called 'out of body' and 'near death' experiences described by many people today. One of the key elements in these experiences is the sense of moving upwards and looking down at one's physical self.

The cloud bore him on through the air, until Black Elk found himself, with the two riders, in a whispering cloudscape, with hills and mountains of cloud rising with majestic beauty from a flat plain, on which a horse was standing. The horse spoke to him. 'Behold me!' it said. 'My life-history you shall see.' Then it turned towards the west, and said, 'Behold them! Their history you shall know.'

Black Elk looked and saw twelve black horses. The horse that had spoken to him then indicated twelve white horses standing to the north, twelve sorrel horses in the east, and twelve buckskins to the south.

At that moment, the sky was filled with horses of all colours.

In the company of these countless horses, Black Elk began to walk across the sky. As he looked about himself in wonder and amazement, he saw all the myriad horses that surrounded him transform themselves, without warning, into animals of every kind, which then fled across the sky towards the four cardinal points from which they had come.

As he continued to walk, the boy became aware of a curious cloud ahead, shaped like a tepee, whose doorway was a rainbow. Through the doorway he could see six old men sitting together in council. These were the Six Grandfathers who had called to him in his previous visions; and now the oldest of them said to him, 'Come right in and do not fear.' There was great kindness in the old man's voice. Black Elk could hear the neighing of the sky-horses all around him, as if cheering him, and so he entered the tepee. The men were indeed old; the boy had the impression that they were as old as the Earth, as old even as the stars.

In a gentle tone, the old man informed Black Elk that he had been called to them so that they might teach him. But this made the boy afraid, for he realised that these beings, the Six Grand-fathers, only appeared to be old men: in reality they were the Powers of the World. They gave him gifts to aid him in the course towards shamanism that had been chosen for him: a bow to destroy his enemies; a sacred herb to heal the sick; a peace pipe with an eagle on the stem; and a living stick with sprouting branches, which seemed to contain all the living things of the Earth.

Black Elk then found himself hovering above three streams, which joined each other to form a vast torrent. Within the mighty flames that gouted from the churning waters, he saw a blue man, whom he perceived to be his enemy, indeed the enemy of all life. Black Elk's bow became a spear, which he hurled into the blue man's heart, killing him. The flames were extinguished, and the land was cured of its sickness. This was the first of the trials that Black Elk would have to go through, in common with other shamans. It should be remembered that, although he did not travel through the sky and meet the Powers of the World in a physical sense, it was experienced by his spirit, his deepest, innermost self; in shamanic cultures, these experiences have just as much validity as what happens in the physical world, if not more so.

Together with the four celestial animal troops, Black Elk swooped down upon a village in a valley, whose people were suffering and dying. And yet, as he passed them, he saw that they were suddenly cured, and were smiling and happy. He heard a voice telling him that it was the power of his celestial gifts, the flowering stick and the peace pipe, that had ended their nation's suffering. Following the instructions of the voice, Black Elk went to the centre of the village and thrust the flowering stick into the ground. Beneath the branches of the tree, all the animals and people came together like relatives, and were happy in each other's company.

Black Elk then led the people away from their village along a road that stretched before them. The boy looked up and saw four ascents ahead, which were the generations he would know in life. All the old people in the line lifted their hands to the sky and began to sing a song, and the sky was filled with the faces of babies. When they came to the end of the first ascent, they made camp in a land filled with green, the holy tree at its centre.

The second ascent was a little steeper, although the land was still green, and as they continued upwards, the people of the village changed into elks and bison, while Black Elk turned into an eagle and soared over them. Towards the end of this ascent, all the animals began to grow restless and afraid, calling out to their chiefs that they were not what they had been, and when they camped Black Elk saw that the leaves had begun to fall from the holy tree.

When they broke camp, the people saw the black road stretching before them, the road of troubles, which they did not want to take. They had no choice but to take this road, however; and as they began the third ascent, great black clouds spread across the sky towards them. As they moved, the animals that the people had become ran here and there, as if uncertain of the way, or as if following their own rules, without regard to the rest of the group. Black Elk could hear winds roaring through the universe 'like wild beasts fighting'.

When they reached the summit of the third ascent, their nation seemed to Black Elk to be in disarray, and when he looked at the holy tree, he could see that it was dying, and the birds that had sung from its branches were now gone. When he looked towards the fourth ascent, he saw that it would be even worse.

As they were about to begin the fourth ascent, the voice spoke again, and this time it sounded as if it were weeping: 'Look there upon your nation.' Black Elk did as he was told, and saw that the animals had become people again; but they were thin and their faces were sharp, and Black Elk knew that they were starving. Worse, the holy tree had vanished. Black Elk wept for the people. Presently, however, he became aware of a 'sacred man' standing to the north of the camp. His entire body was painted red, and he held a spear as he walked into the centre of the camp. The man lay down and rolled around on the ground, and when he got up he was a fat bison. Where this bison stood a sacred herb sprang from the ground, as if to replace the holy tree. As the people watched, the herb sprouted four blossoms, a blue, a white, a scarlet and a yellow.

Only later in life did Black Elk realise the meaning of what had happened. The bison and the herb were gifts from a good spirit, and were the people's strength. But they would lose that strength, and ultimately would find another from the same spirit.

But still the fourth ascent lay ahead, and in the form of an eagle Black Elk soared high above the land, and saw that everything there was dark, torn by violent, battling winds and thunder that sounded like gunfire. The world was filled with smoke and the terrible sounds of women and children screaming. The people ran to their tepees, closing the flaps of their doors against the onrushing storm and the terrified birds it scattered before it.

At that moment, a song of power came to Black Elk, and he sang aloud that he had the power to make the nation live. He found himself on his bay horse again, and in the distance to the west he saw another horse that was nothing but skin and bone.

The voice instructed him to remake the horse. He looked down and saw that he was holding the four-rayed herb in his hand. He did what the voice had bidden him, riding in a circle above the emaciated horse, while the people chanted, calling for the power of the spirits. The emaciated horse neighed and got up, completely restored to health. The now-magnificent stallion galloped off towards the west, his snorting like flashes of lightning, and where his hoofs kicked up dust, the dust became countless black stallions snorting and neighing in unison. Then the horses all stopped and stood in a great circle about their chief, the black stallion that Black Elk had saved with the four-rayed herb. From the north, south, east and west came four beautiful virgins. One held a wooden cup of water, one a white wing, one a sacred pipe and one the nation's hoop. And in the silence of the listening universe, the black stallion raised his head and sang that the horses were coming.

Although the stallion sang this song in a very gentle voice, the soft sound filled the universe, so that everything heard it, and everything could not keep from dancing with the joy of it. The virgins danced, as the other horses circled about.

As Black Elk watched, a cloud passed over his people; but it was a good cloud, which provided them with rain before moving to the east, where it halted beneath a magnificent rainbow. All the horses walked back to their places beyond the summit of the fourth ascent.

Once again accompanied by the riders of the north, south, east and west, Black Elk rode on his own mount towards the east, and a forest-covered chain of mountains. Then he found himself on the highest of the mountains, looking down upon the whole world. As he stood there, he came to understand the true nature of the world and the universe as a single, unified whole. This awakening of understanding, of suddenly becoming aware of the interconnectedness of nature, is an experience common not only in shamanic cultures, but also to all those who undergo spiritual awakenings. It is characterised by the appreciation of the fact that what is done to one person or thing will inevitably have consequences in the wider world, since all people and things are intimately connected to each other.

A voice then instructed him to return to the Six Grandfathers who had given him his gifts. Black Elk now looked down at himself, and realised for the first time that he was painted red all over, while his joints were painted black, with white stripes between them. His bay horse was also painted with lightning stripes. And when he breathed, his breath was lightning.

Now the two men who had first brought Black Elk up from the earth to the heavens reappeared, and beckoned him to follow, turning into four flocks of geese, circling him and calling to each other with sacred voices. He saw the rainbow flaming above the tepee of the Six Grandfathers, built and roofed with cloud and sewed with thongs of lightning; and underneath it were all the wings of the air and under them the animals and men, and they were all rejoicing.

Black Elk's entry into the tepee of the Six Grandfathers was greeted by cheering that came from all over the universe. The Grandfathers all sat facing him, and held out their hands; and behind them he could see a throng of faces of all the people yet to be born. The Grandfathers cried, 'He has triumphed!' The oldest then told him that he had seen the entire universe, and that now he had to return to his own people.

The tepee in which the Six Grandfathers sat now began to sway as if in a great wind, fading and becoming more and more insubstantial. He walked out of the tepee to see that the sun was rising, and suddenly he felt very lonely, for it seemed that now there was no one with him. But a voice said, 'Look back!' He looked and saw that the voice belonged to a great eagle that hovered in the air; and where the cloud-tepee of the Six Grandfathers had been, now stood the mountain at the centre of the world.

Black Elk now found himself standing alone on a vast plain, while the eagle guarded him from on high. In the distance, he could see the village of his people, and towards this he now made his way as quickly as he could, for he was very anxious to be home. When he found his own tepee and looked inside, he saw his parents bending over the sick child that was himself. He entered, and as he did so he heard someone say, 'The boy is coming to; you had better give him some water.'

And then Black Elk sat up.

For several years Black Elk told no one of his complex vision. Although he thought of it often, he was afraid to tell of it; and afraid also because he had no idea how he might fulfil the responsibility to his people that the Six Grandfathers had told him was his. 'I did not know how to do what they wanted me to do,' he told John Neihardt.

His frustration and fear grew worse when he was sixteen years old. He found himself disliking the company of other people, and would ride out alone far from their camp. It seemed that the entire world, the entire universe, was waiting for him to do something, to realise the potential that the Six Grandfathers had shown to him. He was afraid of the animals, afraid of the words they spoke to each other regarding him. He longed for the winter, when the thunderstorms would cease and their voices fall silent. And yet the coyotes still called to each other that it was time, and Black Elk would run from tepee to tepee, trying to escape the voices and their words, until he fell exhausted and slept.

His parents were terribly worried, and feared that he was again suffering from the sickness that had afflicted him a few years earlier. And yet, he could not bring himself to tell them the real reason for his misery, for he was sure they would think him crazy.

When he was seventeen, Black Elk's parents decided to ask an old medicine man named Black Road to see if he could do anything for their son. Black Road took the young man into a tepee and sat alone with him, asking him if he had seen anything that had troubled him. Black Elk could no longer stand to keep the truth to himself, and he told Black Road of the vision he had had.

Although surprised, the old medicine man understood perfectly. He told the youth that it would be necessary for him to perform his vision in a horse dance for his people. Black Road went to see a very old and wise man named Bear Sings, who said he would help in the preparations for Black Elk's horse dance. A crier was sent around the people, and he told them to make camp in a circle at the centre of which Black Road and Bear Sings set up a sacred tepee of bison hide, upon which they painted scenes from Black Elk's vision. They painted a bow and a cup of water on the west side; on the north, white geese and the sacred herb; on the east, the daybreak star and the pipe; and on the south, the flowering stick and the nation's hoop. Over the door of the tepee, they painted a rainbow.

They told Black Elk that he must not eat anything until the horse dance was over, that he had to purify himself in a sweat lodge whose floor was spread with sage, and afterwards to dry himself with sage leaves.

In the evening, Black Road and Bear Sings took Black Elk into the sacred tepee and asked him if he had heard any songs during his vision. He replied that he had, and the old, wise men asked him to teach these songs to them. This he did; it took most of the night, and during this time they heard the thunder rumbling outside. This was taken as a good sign, a sign that the thunder beings were pleased with what they were doing.

Black Elk's parents also helped with the preparations, gathering all the things he would need to perform the horse dance. They gathered four black horses to represent the west; four white horses for the north; four sorrels for the east; and four buckskins for the south. They chose strong, young riders for these horses, and Black Elk himself was given a bay horse to ride, just as he had had in his vision. The Six Grandfathers were represented by the oldest men in the village; and the virgins he had encountered were represented by the village's most beautiful maidens.

Finally, it was time to perform the horse dance. The sixteen horses all faced the sacred tepee, as did the maidens. The horse riders were painted in different ways: the black-horse riders were painted black with blue lightning stripes upon their arms and legs, with white hail spots on their hips; the white-horse riders were painted white with red lightning streaks on their limbs and plumes of white horse hair upon their heads to represent geese;

the sorrel-riders were painted red with black lightning streaks; and the buckskins were painted yellow with black lightning. Black Elk was painted red with black lightning; he wore a black mask with a single eagle feather upon his forehead. His bay horse had red lightning streaks upon its limbs, and on its back, where he sat, was painted an eagle with its wings outstretched. The four maidens wore scarlet buckskin dresses, and their faces were painted red. They wore wreaths of sacred sage, from the front of which hung a single eagle feather.

Black Elk had to stay in the sacred tepee, unseen by anyone but the Six Grandfathers and the maidens, until the horse dance began. The Grandfathers etched a circle in the ground at the centre of the tepee, and across this they drew two lines, one running north to south and one, running east to west. They placed a cup of water and a small bow and arrow on the west side of the circle, and on the east they painted the daybreak star.

Then they gave to the maidens the items they would need: to the maiden of the north they gave the healing herb and a white goose wing; to the maiden of the east they gave the holy pipe; the southern maiden received the flowering stick; and the western maiden was given the nation's hoop. Black Elk himself carried a red stick to represent the sacred arrow, the power of the thunder beings.

The Six Grandfathers then left the sacred tepee and began to sing, announcing the arrival of the riders, beginning with the black-horse riders. The black riders then mounted their horses and turned them to face west. The Grandfathers then announced the white-horse riders, who mounted and faced the north. The red horsemen mounted and faced the east; and the four yellow riders mounted and faced the south.

Black Elk walked out of the sacred tepee, followed the four virgins and mounted his horse and faced the west. The Six Grandfathers then stood behind his horse, and sang that the horse nation of the west was coming to behold him. As the Grandfathers sang the same song of all the other horse troops, each in turn took its place behind them, and all stood facing the west. When all had taken their positions, a dark cloud settled over the camp. Everyone looked up, and the horses stopped their whinnying and prancing. In the distance, thunder growled quietly, as if the sky were clearing its throat. All the horses in the village, and even those in the valley nearby, pricked up their ears and began to paw the earth and neigh. And as he looked at the cloud, Black Elk again saw the sky-tepee built of clouds, with the beautiful rainbow over its doorway and its thongs of lightning, and the Six Grandfathers sitting underneath. He saw himself also, as he had appeared in his vision.

The Six Grandfathers and the Black Elk of the vision all turned to him and held out their hands; and he responded with a prayer. The thundercloud then roared with the voices of the spirits, and a swarm of swallows wheeled and darted through the air above the camp. The people of the village hurried to secure their tepees against the winds.

The thundercloud released its torrent of hail and rain upon the earth, but only a little fell on Black Elk's people. It was a sign that the thunder beings had come in a great crowd to watch the horse dance; and they were pleased with what they saw. The four virgins held up their sacred relics, offering them to the spirits of the west, and as they did so, the people of the village who were sick or sad came forward. Some were cured of their sickness, and those who were sad felt happier, and they began to dance for joy.

The Six Grandfathers began to beat their drums again, and the black-horse riders rode to the west side of the camp, with all the other horse riders following them. When they had reached the western side, they fell behind the buckskin riders, and the white horse troop then led the way to the north side of the village. Then they fell behind the black riders, while the sorrels led the way to the east side of the village; then they fell behind the whites, and the buckskins led the way to the south. Then they too fell back, and the black riders led the way once again to the west. Each time a horse troop reached its quarter, the Six Grandfathers sang of the powers of that quarter, and Black Elk turned his bay horse to face that direction.

The powerful thunder voices within the great dark cloud responded: 'Hey-hey! Hey-hey!' The people of the village responded with the same cry. The spirits of the sky and the people of the earth rejoiced together in the performing of the horse dance. The horse troops repeated their movements around the village four more times, while the Grandfathers sang of the power of each of the four quarters. At each quarter, someone who was sick or sad would approach the four virgins with an offering of red willow bark; and when the virgins received the offering, the person would begin to feel better, and would dance with joy.

On the second course around the village, those with horses of their own mounted them and joined the procession, while others danced on foot behind them.

When they reached the western quarter for the fourth time, they all stopped and faced inward, toward the sacred tepee at the centre of the village. In this new formation the virgins stood first, then Black Elk upon his bay horse and then the Six Grandfathers with eight riders on each side, the sorrels and buckskins on their right, the blacks and whites on their left.

Black Road, the wise old medicine man, took the sacred pipe from the virgin of the east and filled it with red willow bark. He lit it and passed it on, so that everyone in the village might partake.

The horse dance was now over, and Black Elk was so happy that he felt as if he were not walking upon the ground, but above it. His happiness was shared by all the people of the village, many of whom went up to him with gifts and told him that their sick relatives were now feeling much better. He no longer felt fear when the thunderclouds appeared, for now he saw them as relatives. The medicine men, who had not bothered with him before, now came to him to discuss his vision.

From then on, Black Elk always got up early to watch the rising of the daybreak star. Sometimes others in the village would join him, and they would watch it together. And when it rose, they said, together, 'Behold the star of understanding!'

THREE

Wizardry in the Ancient World

'O thou Sun, send me as far over the earth as is my
    pleasure and thine,
and may I make the acquaintance of good beings,
but never hear anything of bad ones, nor they of me.'

APOLLONIUS OF TYANA

Wizards have always been with us. Their shadows stretch across
human history alongside the questions we have always asked
regarding our nature and purpose on Earth, and they walked
serene across the lands of antiquity, attempting to discover the
meaning of human existence, sometimes imparting their knowledge to others along the way. Perhaps the most magically orien-
tated of all the lands of the ancient world was Greece, whose
mystery-shrouded landscape, with its remote mountains, tene-
brous caves and volcanic springs, was a natural theatre in which
magic and legend might grow and develop. The Greek gods
made their homes there: Apollo at Parnassus, Adonis in the vale
of Aphaca, Zeus at Dodona. The gods, goddesses and heroes of
ancient Greece were constantly working their magic. Bacchus,
for instance, could transform a ship and every person and thing
aboard to animals and plants with a wave of his spear: the oars
into serpents, the masts into vines, and the sailors into dolphins

arcing through the sea spray. While Circe turned her lovers into swine, Hermes bestowed life or death with a single stroke of his serpent-staff; those who looked upon Medusa's face were instantly turned to stone, and Perseus passed by unseen in Pluto's helmet of invisibility; Prometheus stole fire from heaven, and Achilles was made invulnerable, apart from his heel, by the waters of the River Styx.

The land contained many places where the worlds of the living and the dead met in subtle and ill-understood ways; where the spirits of those who had passed from the mortal world might be evoked. In places such as Heraclea and Acheron, those who would know the secrets of future times called forth the shades of the dead for fleeting moments during which some clue might be passed from the darkness of the netherworld to the light of living day.

In the month of March, when the flowers of spring revealed themselves and winter passed into memory, the Festival of Flowers was held at Athens, along with the Commemoration of the Dead, whose spirits were believed to rise from below and enter the city once again, wandering through the streets they had known in life, and trying to gain entry to the homes of the living and the temples of the gods. Great care had to be taken to prevent them from succeeding, for the world does not belong to the dead, and is not their rightful dwelling place. The doorways of houses and temples were therefore protected with branches of whitethorn and knotted ropes and pitch.

Perhaps the most famous and ancient of Greek magical practices was the consultation of the Oracles. Just as the more courageous or foolhardy of men attempted to ascertain the future from the words of the dead, others sought the same knowledge through the divine emanations of the Oracles, whose words could influence the actions both of individuals and the state itself. There were many ways in which an Oracle might reveal the course of future events: by means of intoxicating vapours (both natural and artificial), by the drinking of water from mineral springs, or by dreams.

Oracles were to be found throughout the country, but the

most famous were those at Delphi, Dodona, Epidaurus and Trophonius. One of the oldest was the Oracle of Aesculapius, son of Apollo, whose healing powers were transmitted through the dreams of those who slept in the sacred groves surrounding his temple courts at Epidaurus.

The Oracle at Delphi, Apollo himself, was situated on the southern slopes of Mount Parnassus, and people from all walks of life, whether kings or paupers, soldiers or traders, came to ask what the future held for them. The temple stood on the edge of a fiery volcanic fissure, a searing chasm in whose throat danced the flames of the inner earth. Here, the unseen powers of the supernatural world were strong and active. On the very edge of the chasm sat a priestess known as the Pythia, named after the serpent Pytho whom Apollo had slain. As she breathed in the intoxicating vapours rising from a flaming tripod, she would lose control of her body and mind and writhe in a frenzy, her limbs flailing.

The fumes from the tripod were probably narcotics such as hemp or poppy leaves. When she was fully under their influence, the Pythia was said to have been entered by Apollo, who now wrestled with her until she succumbed to his divine influence. In this altered state of consciousness she could now give voice to the god's own words. But those words were not easy to understand, punctuated as they were by moans and gasps, and issuing in staccato rhythms from her frothing mouth. Those who came to her were unable to understand the true meaning behind her ramblings, which had to be interpreted by the attendant priests. These interpreters were highly trained in the decipherment of the bizarre ramblings of the Pythia, which they would transcribe into verse form.

However, no matter how eloquent the poetic forms in which the interpreters presented the Oracle's pronouncements, the problem of ambivalence remained. While the Oracle could never be mistaken (since its utterances had a divine origin), neither was it absolutely right. Its sayings were characterised by double meanings: it always offered two possible outcomes, each containing an element of truth.

When the priest had relayed the Oracle's answer, the suppliant departed to carry out his instructions. If the result coincided with the pronouncement, the Oracle was seen as correct. If the result was not what the suppliant expected, the suppliant re-examined the verses, reading between the lines. He would then become aware of their ambiguous nature, and would see that the result confirmed the alternative meaning that he had initially overlooked.

Eventually, oracular pronouncements were collected and stored in temples and communal archives, and were periodically consulted. Thus, what had previously appeared abstruse might, on a second viewing, become clearer. As a result of this, the validity of the utterances was not bound by time, but became an eternal expression of the god's wisdom. In other words, the prophecy could be fulfilled by the god at any time according to his discretion.

There were many types of questions asked of the Oracles. For instance, a man might ask if it would be wise to marry a certain woman, how many children they would have, whether married life would be agreeable. He might ask how a commercial enterprise would turn out, if it would be profitable or hazardous. In short, all the vicissitudes of ordinary day-to-day life were the subjects of questions asked of the Oracles. Nothing was too important or too mundane to ask the gods.

The oldest of all was the Oracle of Zeus at Dodona, and here the answers to questions regarding the future were not given in the form of spoken words, but rather as signs: the rustling of leaves, the sounds of falling water, the metallic codes of brass bowls moved by the wind. The Oracle was attended by three priestesses, known as Peliades (doves), and existed for two thousand years. It was first consulted by the heroes of the ancient legends, such as Hercules, Achilles and Ulysses.

The Oracle of Trophonius, by contrast, was located underground in a network of caverns where the atmosphere echoed to the sound of hidden waters, and swam with subterranean mists and vapours. Here, those wishing to know of the future would lie down and sleep, sometimes for several days, until they emerged in an altered state of consciousness, and were questioned by the attendant priests. Usually they told of horrific visions encountered in their long sleep, which resulted in a dreadful melancholy. So common was this effect, that if a man were particularly sad, a common saying was that he had been sleeping in the cave of Trophonius.

The Oracles were a means of communing with the gods, and as such were a form of high magic. It was not until after the Persian Wars that low magic or sorcery became known to the Greeks. The concept of good and evil demons, who could be contacted and compelled to perform services for humans, was imported following the invasion by Persia; and in Thessaly in particular, sorcerers and sorceresses roamed far and wide, performing acts of strange magic, such as the creation of potions for love and death. In *The Golden Ass*, Apuleius writes that sorceries and enchantments were practised most frequently in Thessaly. He describes how nothing there was as it appeared to be: it was a place of nightmare, where men were transformed into living stones, into birds and running waters. He goes on to describe how statues and buildings were capable of movement, and how oxen and other beasts were endowed with human speech, and spoke of strange things.

The land was home to many sorceresses, including Circe, and the arch-sorceress Medea, about whom many dreadful tales were told, and who was accomplished in all the evil arts. Hecate, also, was well known and feared. She was the moon-goddess, who originally possessed the heavenly powers along with Zeus, but who later became a truly terrible figure, synonymous with the darkness of night and the world of the dead. The three-headed Hecate was followed everywhere she went by horrible supernatural creatures, including hell hounds and poisonous serpents. She was custodian of the mysteries of life and death, and was worshipped in the dead of night in ceremonies illuminated only by the baleful, flickering flames of torches. At crossroads and other lonely places, small cakes and lizard masks, honey, sacrificed dogs and black lambs were left to honour her, and to beg her not to send her hideous minions to trouble the homes of the living.

Throughout Greece, people sought potions and spells to kill an enemy or secure the love of another. Of course, this resulted in many people seeking magical protection from evil spells, for there were numerous tales of dreadful things happening to those who went without protection. Should misfortune or death befall one, it was considered highly likely that somewhere, in the darkness of the night, a wizard or sorceress had fashioned a wax image of the victim and performed all manner of symbolic tortures upon it. Other practitioners of evil magic favoured different methods, such as taking a lead tablet with the name of the victim inscribed upon it, piercing it with a nail, and burying it in a tomb or other secret place where the laws of nature gave way before other, darker laws.

One of the most powerful forms of magic was Orphic Magic, named after Orpheus, the beautiful worker of wonders, whose exquisite music gave him beneficent control over the worlds of men, animals and plants. He was also a powerful necromancer, who succeeded in retrieving his wife Eurydice from Hades, but lost her just as they were about to return to earth by disobeying the injunction not to gaze upon her beautiful face until they had reached safety. The Thracian women were so enraged by his loss of Eurydice that they ripped him to pieces, and his head was eventually washed up on the shores of the island of Lesbos, where it became an Oracle. People from all over the known world came to hear the words spoken by the disembodied head, this strangest of Oracles. Not only prophecies, but also many magical formulae issued from the head of Orpheus, which were written down upon tablets.

While he is remembered today as a master geometrician and philosopher, Pythagoras was also credited with being a powerful magician, with the ability to appear in two places at the same time. He also possessed the ability to tame wild animals by whispering in their ears, and to call eagles and other birds to alight in his hands.

Greek magic revolved around the Mysteries, secret initiation rites that granted admission to different religious cults. They were held at periodic intervals, and were associated with the different deities. Three of the most famous were the Samothracian, Bacchic and Eleusinian Mysteries. The Mysteries had three trials, by water, air and fire, and their sacred emblems were the phallus, the egg and the serpent, all of which were symbols of fertility, of the generation of life.

The Samothracian Mysteries involved the worship of four mysterious beings: Axieros, the mother; her son, Axiocersos; her daughter, Axiocersa; and her grandchild, Casindos, who was believed to have created the Universe. The ceremonies probably celebrated the creation of the world, and the harvest that maintained human life. The goddess Cybele, who represented the Earth, its fields and cities, was also worshipped in the Samothracian Mysteries; and her priests held their ceremonies in caves where they danced wildly, banging their swords against their shields.

The Bacchic Mysteries revolved around the god of the vine. Bacchus was attended by women known as Bacchantes, who shrieked and struck cymbals together in the noisy abandon of their worship, during which they would give themselves over to uncontrollable frenzies.

Greatest of all, however, were the Eleusinian Mysteries. The rites were steeped in secrecy, and very little is known of their true nature, beyond the likelihood that they involved the legend of Demeter, the corn-goddess, and her daughter Persephone, and the fact that they were held in the spring and the autumn. Initiates into the Eleusinian Mysteries were required to undergo a long period of purification before being instructed in the mysteries themselves. Following this, the initiates were shown certain very sacred symbols, before being crowned with garlands, signifying the joy of being in the presence of the divine.

In addition to the Oracles, there was also a group of men known as Interpreters, whose responsibility it was to read the future through the observation of flights of birds, the shape of entrails of slaughtered men and beasts, and so on. As might be expected, these men were highly sought after by military leaders, and generals would often take them on military campaigns, so that they might predict the outcomes of engagements. It should also be no surprise that this profession was followed by innumerable confidence tricksters, who took easy advantage of people's desire to know the future.

One of the most celebrated wizards of the ancient world we have described was Apollonius of Tyana.

According to the whisperings of legend, great wonders attended the birth of Apollonius in the small town of Tyana in present-day Turkey. One such legend relates to his mother, who was walking in a meadow shortly before giving birth to him. She lay down to sleep on the grass, and as she slept, some wild swans descended upon her, crying and beating their wings. So great was this sudden shock that it induced labour, and she gave premature birth to Apollonius right there in the meadow. The legend has it that the swans knew that a great wanderer, whose soul was as pure as their white plumage, was about to be born, and had come to attend him.

Apollonius of Tyana was born around 4 BC at Tyana in Cappadocia, about 100 kilometres north of Tarsus. At the time, this region was home to many different religions. Zoroastrian wizards travelled widely throughout the area, teaching the doctrine of the Fire Aeon of Aries, and the necessity of transferring the sacred knowledge into the new Age of Pisces. To the south, in the Comana region, the powerful nature goddess Ma was worshipped; while to the west, Zeus had an important temple.

At the age of sixteen, Apollonius began his education at the Temple of Asclepius at Aegae, which is north of Mount Olympus and is now the city of Edessa. It is here that he became a devotee of the sect of Pythagoras and began his training in the art of becoming immortal. It is said that Apollonius was gifted with exceptional physical beauty and great intelligence; indeed, such were these qualities in him that a saying arose in Cappadocia: 'Whither do you hurry? Are you on your way to see the young man?'

Not only was he beautiful; he was also rich, his father being one of the wealthiest men in the region. He thus spent his childhood in considerable luxury, with his every want catered for. This upbringing resulted in his only flaw, although it could be considered a minor one. He tended towards the maintenance of an aristocratic bearing, and was always anxious to call upon the monarch of whichever country he visited before doing anything else.

Today, the ways of education in philosophy are not as they were then (although many a modern undergraduate might wish that they were); in those far-off days, the students of Tarsus would relax in orange groves on the banks of the Cydnus River and discuss the philosophy of Plato and Pythagoras with young women who wore clinging, brightly coloured tunics. Much wine would be drunk, and frequently the tunics would be allowed to fall to the ground as the fragrant delights of physical love drifted among the trees in the heat of the afternoon. Apollonius, however, decided that it was far better to forsake the love and wine, for he felt that each in its own way interfered with the successful honing of the intellect and the cultivation of the spirit. He decided that his life would be one of physical chastity, allowing him to devote himself exclusively to the development of mind and spirit.

Apollonius continued his education in the company of his Epicurean teacher Euxenes. People came from far and wide, from Greece, Syria and Alexandria to consult the philosopher-priests of the Pythagorean school at Aegae. Powerful magic was practised there; the priests of Aegae healed by the laying on of hands, and were adept at the interpretation of dreams. At the core of their magic were the Orphic Mysteries, and the school itself constituted a secret community whose members cultivated knowledge of music, geometry and astronomy as the principal means by which reality might be understood. They taught the doctrine of metempsychosis, the transmigration of souls through successive human bodies, and the importance of courage and temperance in the development of one's spiritual awareness. Their teachings were characterised by a mixture of scientific principles and occult mysticism: they understood the power and significance of numbers in the mechanisms of Nature, and also used magical incantations to communicate with the dead.

At the Temple of Asclepius, Apollonius demonstrated his impressive gifts of both healing and clairvoyance. Euxenes was somewhat bemused by the young man's asceticism, and questioned his vegetarianism and abstinence from alcohol, claiming that the pleasures of life were not necessarily barriers to the cultivation of spiritual wisdom. In spite of their disagreements, Apollonius was extremely fond of his hedonistic teacher, and bought him a villa near Aegae at which he might discuss philosophy with his friends while enjoying sumptuous meals, just as Plato had done at Agathon's banquet.

Apollonius possessed an insatiable desire for knowledge, which drove him to travel throughout the East, performing miracles (so it was said) wherever he went. One of the stories of his talents as a magician tells how at Ephesus he foresaw the approach of a terrible plague, but was not believed by the people of the city. When the plague was upon them, they remembered what Apollonius had said, and begged him to help them.

Apollonius pointed to a poor beggar, maimed and wretched, who was sitting in the street, and told the people that here was the cause of their woes. The beggar, he said, had brought the pestilence upon them; he was an enemy of all that was good, and should be stoned to death immediately. The people of Ephesus were shocked by this announcement, and were extremely reluctant to harm the beggar. And yet, when they looked at his face they became aware of something frightful in the beggar's expression. Without further hesitation, they took up stones and pummelled him to death with such ferocity that he lay completely covered by a mound of stones. When the stones were removed, the people found not a man, but an enormous black dog, an infernal being, which had been the true cause of the pestilence.

Apollonius' magical talents also extended to raising people

from the dead, which feat he performed for a young woman of noble family in Rome. Halting the funeral procession, he cried, 'Set down the bier, and I will dry the tears being shed for this maid.' A few moments later, the girl sat up and rejoined her family. When asked how such miracles were possible, he replied:

> There is no death of anything save in appearance. That which passes over from essence to nature seems to be birth, and what passes over from nature to essence seems to be death. Nothing really is originated, and nothing ever perishes; but only now comes into sight and now vanishes. It appears by reason of the density of matter, and disappears by reason of the tenuity of essence. But it is always the same, differing only in motion and condition.

He was also able to recognise vampires. In this case his friend, Menippus of Corinth, was betrothed to a beautiful woman. Apollonius' clairvoyance alerted him to her true nature, and although he tried to warn his friend, Menippus refused to believe him. On the day of the ceremony, Apollonius arrived and through the force of his magical will caused the wedding guests and decorations, which had been but illusions, to vanish, leaving only the young woman, who was forced to admit that she was a vampire.

The only source of information on Apollonius that has survived from antiquity is the biography written by Philostratus at the request of Julia, mother of the Emperor Severus. The biography was apparently compiled from an earlier work, the memoirs of Damis the Assyrian, one of Apollonius' disciples. In his *Encyclopaedia of Occultism*, Lewis Spence notes:

> The work is largely a romance; fictitious stories are often introduced, and the whole account is mystical and symbolical. Nevertheless it is possible to get a glimpse of the real character of Apollonius beyond the literary artifices of the writer. The purpose of the philosopher of Tyana seems to

have been to infuse into paganism a morality more practical combined with a more transcendental doctrine. He himself practised a very severe asceticism, and supplemented his own knowledge by revelations from the gods.

It was after hearing the stories concerning the Buddhist priest Zarmaros of Bargosa that Apollonius decided to travel to India. Zarmaros had travelled to Athens some years previously as part of an Indian mission bringing gifts for the Emperor Augustus. While in the city, the old man declared that it was finally time for him to leave his life behind. He had a funeral pyre built in a public square, climbed upon it and had it set alight, much to the astonishment of the assembled Athenians. Zarmaros' utter contempt for death and physical suffering fascinated Apollonius, and he decided that he must visit the home country of the famous priest.

During his journey, which he made on foot, Apollonius made a point of visiting the places that were sacred to the gods. In the region of Antioch he came upon a temple of Apollo, and was immediately captivated by it and the beauty of its surroundings. His admiration was interrupted by the arrival of a solitary peasant-priest, who had just finished tending to his land. The man offered the visitor shelter for the night, which Apollonius readily accepted: he intended to return to the temple just before sunrise, since he believed that communion with the gods was best conducted just prior to the birth of the new day.

As Apollonius knelt in prayer in the temple the next day, the peasant-priest brought to him the treasure it was his responsibility to guard, and which he had decided Apollonius was worthy to receive. The treasure consisted of several thin sheets of copper, on which were engraved a number of curious symbols and diagrams. The peasant-priest said that he was unable to divine their meaning, but Apollonius was able to decipher them, and saw that they were a set of directions leading to the monastery of the Immortals on Mount Kailas in Tibet.

Apollonius then visited the city of Nineveh, where he discovered amid half-buried ruins a strange statue of an unknown goddess with horns sprouting from her head. Nearby sat a youth who introduced himself as Damis, and who evidently saw something of the divine in the visitor, for he attached himself to Apollonius from that moment on, and never left his side.

According to Philostratus, the companions then set off for Babylon, where they stayed for a while to consult with the magicians who lived there, and from whom Apollonius learned much concerning the Chaldean mysteries. The King of Babylon befriended him and provided him with camels and a guide for the continuance of his journey. Thereafter the trek became more arduous. They climbed gigantic, cloud-veiled mountains, Apollonius spurring his new friend on with the words, 'When the soul is without blemish, it can rise far above the highest mountains.'

Damis was intelligent enough, but not particularly inclined to the consideration of spiritual matters, a state of affairs that Apollonius periodically tried to remedy during their journey. One day, during the ascent of a mountain, he said to his companion: 'Tell me, Damis, where were we yesterday?'

'On the plain,' replied Damis.

'And where are we today?'

'Unless I am mistaken,' he responded, 'we are on the Caucasus.'

Apollonius nodded and continued, 'Then yesterday we were *below*; today we are *above*. In what respect do these two conditions differ?'

Damis replied, 'They differ in this respect: that yesterday's journey has been made by many travellers; but this day's journey is made by the few.'

It was in this way that Apollonius was able to draw his friend's attention to the spiritual path, and the few people who manage to travel successfully upon it.

The travellers crossed the Indus, and then followed the course of the Ganges for some days. Presently, they found themselves in a strange landscape that seemed to shift and alter, so that the path by which they had just come seemed to have vanished. A strange, writhing fog covered the ground, making it even harder to keep their bearings. Damis was nonplussed, but Apollonius knew that at last they had reached their goal: the country of the Wise Men. Later, he would claim, 'I have seen men who inhabit the earth, yet do not live on it, who are protected on all sides though they have no means of defence, and who nevertheless possess only what all men possess.'

Standing on the summit of a steep hill stood the monastery of the Wise Men. Apollonius saw it, but Damis could see only the mist that enveloped it. Presently they became aware of a young Indian approaching them from out of the mist. The Wise Men were well aware of their visitors' presence, and so the young man, who wore a caduceus upon his brow, greeted them in Greek. He conducted them to the leader of the Wise Men, Iarchas. Apollonius asked him if he might be allowed to stay at the monastery and be instructed in philosophy.

Iarchas replied that he would gladly instruct the visitor. 'I will, with all my heart, for the communication of knowledge is much more becoming the character of philosophy than the concealment of what ought to be known.' He invited Apollonius to ask him whatever questions he pleased.

Recalling the words engraved above the entrance to the Temple of Apollo at Delphi ('Man, know thyself'), Apollonius responded, 'Do you know yourselves?'

Iarchas answered, 'We know all things because we know ourselves. For there is not one among us who would have been admitted to the study of philosophy had he not had that previous knowledge.'

'As what, then, do you consider yourselves?'

'As gods,' was the reply.

'And why gods?'

'Because we are good men.'

When it was time for Apollonius to leave the monastery, Iarchas gave him seven rings, each of which was to be worn on a certain day of the week. Apollonius said to the ascended masters, 'I came to you by land, and you have opened to me not only the way of the sea but, through your wisdom, the way to heaven. All these things I will bring back to the Greeks, and if I have not drunk in vain of the cup of Tantalus I shall continue to speak with you as though you were present. Farewell, excellent philosophers.'

The masters walked with them to the edge of the valley of meditation, and gave them white camels on which to journey home.

Wherever Apollonius travelled, legend followed in his wake. Among his many accomplishments, he acted as counsellor to the Emperor Vespasian; recognised the spirit of a much-loved king in a gentle and tame lion that refused to eat meat; restored reason to a madman who had intended to marry a statue; exorcised a sexually obsessed demon from the body of a man who attacked every woman he met; and cured a man who had been bitten by a rabid dog.

Apollonius taught the alchemical system of the four elements: earth, air, fire and water; and also taught that there was a fifth element, ether, or prana, which was the substance the Immortals inhaled to maintain their eternal life. The Universe, he said, is a living being, and everything in it, whether animate or inanimate, possesses consciousness. If we believe this, then we are in a better position to apprehend the sacred aspects of reality, and thus will be able to accelerate our spiritual evolution.

The manner of Apollonius' death is shrouded in mystery. There are a number of contradictory accounts of his final moments. Some say he simply disappeared without a trace; others that he vanished while on his deathbed; still others that he simply walked out of his house at Ephesus one evening and was never seen again, or vanished while meditating in a temple of Dictynna. Several Roman emperors who had admired him attempted to investigate his disappearance, but none found any satisfactory answers.

As might be expected, Apollonius provoked as much antipathy and consternation as admiration, especially among Christians, who had little choice but to compare him with his contemporary, Jesus Christ. Apollonius performed many miracles, as did Jesus, but the Greeks refused to call them miracles, maintaining instead that they were merely expressions of the ill-understood laws of nature. This caused Justin Martyr, the great Church Father of the second century, to ask:

> How is it that the talismans of Apollonius have power over certain members of creation, for they prevent, as we see, the fury of the waves, the violence of the winds, and the attacks of wild beasts. And whilst Our Lord's miracles are preserved by tradition alone, those of Apollonius are most numerous, and actually manifested in present facts, so as to lead astray all beholders.

Philostratus, whose account of Apollonius' life is the only extant original source, was surely perfectly aware of the antipathy of Christianity to his subject, and this may in fact have spurred him on in his work. He was, after all, a member of the Pythagorean School, like Apollonius, and it must have given him great satisfaction to describe the intellectual and spiritual achievements of his illustrious fellow Pythagorean. Philostratus writes:

> Some consider him as one of the Magi, because he conversed with the Magi of Babylon and the Brahmans of India and the Gymnosophists of Egypt. But even his wisdom is reviled as being acquired by the magic art, so erroneous are the opinions formed of him. Whereas Empedocles and Pythagoras and Democritus, though they conversed with the same Magi, and advanced many paradoxical sentiments, have not fallen under the like imputation. Even Plato, who travelled in Egypt, and blended with his doctrines many opinions collected there from the priests and prophets, incurred not such a suspicion, though envied above all men on account of his superior wisdom.

Although he was reviled by Christians as an evil sorcerer, it is more accurate to remember Apollonius of Tyana as one of the greatest of history's wise and benign wizards. He taught the immortality of the soul, and the universality of the mind; however, he was reluctant to dwell too much upon these questions, concluding that ultimate truths could only be experienced directly, saying, 'When the body is exhausted, the soul soars in ethereal space, full of contempt for the harsh, unhappy slavery it has suffered. But what are these things to you? You will know them when you are no more.'

What was that strange and fantastic land that Apollonius of Tyana visited? Who were the wise adepts from whom he learned so much? Could there possibly have existed such a profoundly spiritual place in some mysterious and hidden corner of the globe, a phantom kingdom in which the soul of humanity was enshrined and cared for ... and might such a place exist still?

In the late 1970s the writer Andrew Tomas published his book *Shambhala: Oasis of Light*. Based on many years of study of the myths and legends of the Far East, the book is an eloquent argument in favour of the actual existence of a realm of potent magical and spiritual power. In support of his argument, Tomas cites the writings of ancient China, which refer to Nu and Kua, the 'Asiatic prototypes of Adam and Eve' and their birthplace in the Kun Lun Mountains of Central Asia. It is not clear why such a desolate and forbidding place should be regarded as the Chinese equivalent of the Garden of Eden rather than, for instance, the altogether more salubrious regions around the Yangtse Valley. It is quite possible, however, that the Gobi Desert was once a land-locked sea surrounded by fertile land.

The Kun Lun Mountains are very important in Chinese mythology, since it is here that the Immortals are said to live, ruled by Hsi Wang Mu, the Queen Mother of the West. Also known as Kuan Yin, the goddess of mercy, she is said to live in a fabulous palace built of jade, surrounded by a vast garden in which grows the Peach Tree of Immortality. Only the wisest and most virtuous of human beings are permitted to visit the garden and eat the fruit, which appears only once every 6,000 years.

It is the responsibility of Hsi Wang Mu to guide humanity

towards wisdom and compassion; and the Immortals who aid her are said to possess perfect, ageless bodies, to have the ability to travel anywhere in the Universe, and to be able to live on the planets of other star systems. As Tomas notes, whether the ancient Chinese believed that the Immortals could travel in space in their physical bodies or by projecting their minds, this is still a remarkable concept, since it is based on an acceptance of the plurality of inhabited worlds in the Cosmos.

There are many references in the ancient Chinese texts to the attempts by people to cross the Gobi Desert to the Kun Lun Mountains. The most famous of these spiritual adventurers is the great philosopher Lao Tzu (*c.* sixth century BC), author of the *Tao Te Ching*, who is said to have made the journey towards the end of his life. The Vatican archives also contain many reports made by Catholic missionaries concerning deputations from the emperors of China to the spiritual beings living in the mountains. These beings are the 'mind-born' gods whose bodies are composed of elementary atomic matter, and who are able to live anywhere in the Universe, even at the centres of stars.

The people of India also believe in the existence of a place of spiritual wisdom. They call it Kalapa, and believe that it lies in a region north of the Himalayas, in Tibet. Indian tradition holds that the Gobi Desert was once a great sea, which contained an island called Sweta-Dvipa (White Island). The great Yogis who once lived there are believed to live still in the high mountains and deep valleys that once formed the island. This island has been identified by Orientalists with the Isle of Shambhala of Puranic literature, which is said to stand at the centre of a lake of nectar.

In the seventeenth century, two Jesuit missionaries, Stephen Cacella and John Cabral, recorded the existence of Chang Shambhala, as described to them by the lamas of Shigatse, where Cacella lived for twenty-three years. Chang Shambhala means Northern Shambhala, which differentiates it from the town called Shamballa, north of Benares, India. Nearly two centuries later, a Hungarian philologist named Csoma de Körös, who spent four years in a Buddhist monastery in Tibet, claimed that

Chang Shambhala lay between 45° and 50° north latitude, beyond the River Syr Daria.

The ancient cultures of the East preserve many legends of a spiritual centre, a sacred region whose immortal magicians secretly guide the evolution of humanity. In her fascinating book *Shambhala: The Fascinating Truth Behind the Myth of Shangri-la*, writer Victoria Le Page describes this wondrous realm thus:

> ... [Somewhere] beyond Tibet, among the icy peaks and secluded valleys of Central Asia, there lies an inaccessible paradise, a place of universal wisdom and ineffable peace called Shambhala ... It is inhabited by adepts from every race and culture who form an inner circle of humanity secretly guiding its evolution. In that place, so the legends say, sages have existed since the beginning of human history in a valley of supreme beatitude that is sheltered from the icy arctic winds and where the climate is always warm and temperate, the sun always shines, the gentle airs are always beneficent and nature flowers luxuriantly.

Only those with pure hearts may find this place; others, less idealistically motivated, risk an icy grave if they attempt to find it. Here, want, evil, violence and injustice do not exist. The inhabitants possess both magical powers and advanced technology, and devote themselves to the study of the arts and sciences. The concept of the hidden spiritual centre of the world is to be found in Hinduism, Buddhism, Taoism, shamanism and other ancient traditions. In the Bön religion of pre-Buddhist Tibet, Shambhala is also called Olmolungring and Dejong. In Tibetan Buddhism the Shambhalic tradition is enshrined within the Kalachakra texts, which are said to have been taught to the King of Shambhala by the Buddha before being returned to India.

There has, of course, been a great deal of speculation as to the exact whereabouts of Shambhala (it is unlikely to lie at Körös' map coordinates). Some esotericists believe that Shambhala has a real physical presence in a secret location here on Earth, while others prefer to see it as existing on a higher spiritual plane, perhaps in another dimension of spacetime coterminous with our own. Interestingly, there are a number of cases on record in which people have experienced visions of a place bearing a marked resemblance to the fabled Shambhala. Victoria Le Page cites one such case, which was investigated by a Dr Raynor Johnson, who gathered several hundred first-hand accounts in the 1960s of mystical experiences. The case involved a young Australian woman, who was referred to as L.C.W.

At the age of twenty-one, L.C.W. began to travel to a place she came to know as the Night School. She would fly there in her sleep, and while there she would join other people in dance exercises, which she later recognised as being similar to the dervish exercises taught by the philosopher George Gurdjieff. L.C.W. had no idea where the Night School was, but she went there many times over a period of several years, eventually graduating to a different class, where she was taught spiritual lessons from a great book of wisdom. It was only years later, when she began to take a serious interest in mystical literature, that L.C.W. realised that the Night School must have been Shambhala.

L.C.W. also had many even stranger visions in which she saw what appeared to be a gigantic mast or antenna, extending from Earth deep into interstellar space. The base of this antenna was in the Tien Shan Mountains, which are traditionally associated with Shambhala. She approached the antenna in the company of an invisible guide, and saw that it was actually an immense pillar of energy whose branches were paths leading to other worlds, other times and other regions of the Universe. In addition to the antenna functioning as a gateway for souls from Earth to travel to other times and places, 'she believed souls from other systems in space could enter the earth sphere by the same route, carrying their own spiritual influences with them'.

Our knowledge of the Shambhalic tradition in the West has come mainly from Orientalist scholars such as Helena Blavatsky, René Guénon, Louis Jacolliot, Saint-Yves d'Alveydre and, perhaps most importantly, Nicholas Roerich.

Born in St Petersburg, Russia in 1874, Nicholas Roerich came from a distinguished family whose ability to trace its origins to the Vikings of the tenth century inspired his early interest in archaeology. This interest led in turn to a lifelong devotion to art, and after attending the St Petersburg Academy of Fine Art, Roerich went to Paris to study. While he was on a visit to America, the Russian Revolution occurred, and he found himself unable to return to his homeland.

In 1923–26, Roerich led an expedition to Mongolia and Tibet, crossing the Gobi Desert to the Altai Mountains. It was during this expedition that his party had a most unusual experience. By the summer of 1926, Roerich had established a camp with his son, Dr George Roerich, and several Mongolian guides in the Shara-gol Valley near the Humboldt Mountains. Roerich had just built a white *stupa* (or shrine) dedicated to Shambhala and the shrine was consecrated in August in a ceremony that was witnessed by several invited lamas.

Two days later, the party watched as a huge black bird wheeled through the sky above them. This, however, was not what astonished them, for far beyond the black bird, high up in the cloudless sky, they clearly saw a golden spheroidal object moving from the Altai Mountains to the north at fantastic speed. Veering sharply to the south-west, the golden object disappeared beyond the Humboldt Mountains. The Mongolian guides began shouting to each other in great excitement. One of the lamas turned to Roerich and told him that the golden orb was the sign of Shambhala, meaning that the lords of that realm approved of his mission of exploration.

Later, another lama asked Roerich if there had been a perfume on the air at the time of the sighting. When Roerich replied that there had, the lama told him that he was under the protection of the King of Shambhala, Rigden Jye-Po, that the great black bird was his enemy, but that he was protected by a 'Radiant form of Matter'. The lama added that anyone who saw the golden sphere would be well advised to follow the direction in which it flew, for in that direction lay Shambhala.

The exact purpose of the expedition (aside from exploration) was never made entirely clear by Roerich, but many esotericists have claimed that he was on a mission to return a certain sacred object to the King's Tower at the centre of Shambhala. According to Andrew Tomas, this object was a fragment of the fabled Chintamani Stone, which, as legend has it, was brought to Earth by an extraterrestrial being. (It is rumoured that the fragment Roerich was returning to the Tower had been in the possession of the League of Nations, of which Roerich was a respected member.)

The strange mission upon which Nicholas Roerich is said to have embarked illustrates how the legends surrounding Shambhala as the magical power centre of the Earth have survived through the centuries. In truth, they have lost none of their ability to fascinate, and to galvanise the imagination with their adventure, danger and exoticism. They stand as testaments to the significance in modern times of the magic that was taken for granted in the ancient world.

FOUR

The Alchemist

'This much concerning the revelation of our stone is, we doubt not, enough for the Sons of the Doctrine. The strength thereof, shall never become corrupted but the same, when it is placed in the fire, shall be increased. If you seek to dissolve, it shall be dissolved; but if you would coagulate, it shall be coagulated. Behold, no one is without it, and yet all do need it! There are many names given to it, and yet it is called by one only, while, if need be, it is concealed. It is also a stone and not a stone, spirit, soul, and body; it is white, volatile, concave, hairless, cold, and yet no one can apply the tongue with impunity to its surface. If you wish that it should fly, it flies; if you say that it is water, you speak the truth; if you say that it is not water, you speak falsely. Do not then be deceived by the multiplicity of names, but rest assured that it is one thing, into which nothing alien is added.'

GUGLIELMO GRATAROLI, WRITING ON THE
PHILOSOPHER'S STONE, *TURBA PHILOSOPHORUM*

Among the chief concerns of the wizards of the last millennium was the practice of alchemy, an ancient art of mysterious origin that sought the transmutation of base metals such as lead into silver and gold. Opinion is divided among scholars as to whether alchemy originated in ancient Egypt, or China around the fifth century BC.

The origin of the word 'alchemy' is open to debate, but the occult historian Lewis Spence suggested that the likeliest derivation is from the Arabic *al* = the and *kimya* = chemistry, which in turn derives from the late Greek *chemeia* = chemistry. He notes, however, that it could also derive from the Egyptian word *khemeia*, referring to 'the preparation of the black ore', which was believed to be the principal ingredient in the transmutation of metals.

The early alchemists were artisans rather than scientists in the modern sense of the word, and they expended much effort on trying to conceal the exact nature of their experiments, for instance, referring to the materials they used by astrological names. At the centre of alchemy, of course, stands the Philosopher's Stone, a mysterious substance said to possess the power to transform base metal into gold, and also to halt the ageing process and restore youth.

In fact, the alchemist has three goals: to discover a process whereby base metals might be transformed into gold and silver (the Philosopher's Stone); to discover a substance that will prolong life indefinitely (the Elixir of Life); and to discover a means to manufacture, artificially, human life (the resulting entity is known as a homunculus).

The alchemists' research led them to believe that Nature was divided into four elements: the dry, the moist, the warm and the cold. In addition, Nature was also divisible into the male and female principles. In practising his art, the alchemist must maintain an honest and truthful disposition, and above all be patient. The basis of alchemy is the belief that the world naturally strives towards the production of gold; other metals occur, as it were, by accident, the by-products of an environment that is imperfect. Alchemists sought to understand the processes by which metals are created in the earth, processes that depend on the interaction of sulphur (male) and mercury (female), together with a substance, sometimes known as 'the Light', which acts upon matter to perfect it. If this sounds a little vague, it is nothing compared to the alchemical process itself, which is so complex, and couched in such arcane language, as to be completely impenetrable.

Numerous alchemical texts refer to processes of 'purgation', 'dissolution' and 'congelation' of various bizarre substances, which become 'spiritualised' through sublimation.

While some commentators on the subject have claimed that the fundamental intention behind the practice of alchemy is the correlative purification of the human spirit, this is not the case. The main goal of the alchemists was always the production of gold. However, it should be noted that only those of a righteous and pious nature had any chance of success: the discovery of the great secret of alchemy depended very much upon instruction by God.

The great magician and alchemist Paracelsus developed a recipe for producing a homonculus. Certain alchemical substances must be placed in a glass phial, and deposited in a pile of horse dung for forty days. This is enough to create the life principal within the phial, but much more work is required. The living, moving thing within the bottle is an artificial human being, but it is one without physical substance, and is thus transparent. The homonculus must be kept in the dung heap, and be fed for forty weeks with the essence *(see below)* of human blood. At the end of this time, the phial will contain a living child, indistinguishable (apart from his reduced size) from those born naturally.

Paracelsus was a striking and picturesque figure in the history of the occult arts and sciences, and was a keen practitioner of alchemy, not to mention the most original medical thinker of the sixteenth century. His works were a considerable influence on Mary Shelley's Gothic masterpiece of 1818, *Frankenstein*, and although those works were unorthodox and inaccurate by today's standards, they strongly influenced the development of chemistry as an empirical science.

Born in 1493 at Eisiedeln, Switzerland, his full name was Philippus Aureolus Theophrastus Bombastus von Hohenheim. He was known as Theophrastus until he graduated from college, when he renamed himself Paracelsus ('above' or 'beyond Celsus'), which reflected his somewhat egotistical belief that he was greater than the renowned first-century Roman physician Celsus.

The only son of a well-known but somewhat impoverished German doctor and chemist, Paracelsus moved with his father to Villach in southern Austria, following the death of his mother. There the boy attended the Bergschule, where his father taught chemical theory and practice. Pupils at the Bergschule were trained as overseers and analysts for mining operations in gold, tin and mercury, as well as iron, alum and copper-sulphate ores. It was during this period that the young Paracelsus listened in fascination to the miners' talk of metals that 'grow' in the earth, watched the mysterious transformations in the great smelting vats, and wondered if one day he might achieve the alchemist's dream of discovering how to transmute lead into gold.

In 1507 at the age of fourteen, having gained the insights into metallurgy and chemistry that laid the foundations of his later discoveries in chemotherapy, Paracelsus embarked on a journey across Europe, seeking famous teachers at one university after another. During the next five years, he is said to have attended the universities of Basel, Tÿbingen, Vienna, Wittenberg, Leipzig, Heidelberg and Cologne, but was deeply disappointed with them all. With his typical acerbic wit, he later wrote that he wondered how 'the high colleges managed to produce so many high asses'. Needless to say, this attitude did not endear him to his teachers. Elsewhere, he wrote, 'The universities do not teach all things, so a doctor must seek out old wives, gypsies, sorcerers, wandering tribes, old robbers, and such outlaws and take lessons from them. A doctor must be a traveller ... Knowledge is experience.'

After graduating from the University of Vienna with the baccalaureate in medicine in 1510, he attended the University of Ferrara, where he was delighted to find that the medicine of Galen and the medieval Arab teachers was heavily criticised. At Ferrara, he was free to express his contempt for the prevailing view that the stars and planets controlled all the parts of the human body. He later claimed to have received his doctoral degree from Ferrara in 1516, although university records are missing from that year.

While Paracelsus found the intellectual atmosphere at Ferrara agreeable, a man of such ferocious intelligence and independence of mind could not feel comfortable for long in any seat of learning. In addition, his studies in necromancy did not go down well with the authorities. Shortly after taking his degree, he set off across Europe once again, visiting almost every country, including England, Ireland and Scotland. During a spell in Russia, he was captured by the Tartars and brought before the Grand Cham, at whose court he became a great favourite. He accompanied the Cham's son on a journey from China to Constantinople, where he learned the secret of the universal dissolvent (the *alkahest*) from an Arabian alchemist.

Ultimately, his restless wanderings took him to Egypt, Arabia and the Holy Land. Throughout his long journey, he had sought out the most learned practitioners of alchemy, to discover the most effective means of medical treatment and, more importantly, to discover 'the latent forces of nature' and how to use them. He wrote, 'He who is born in imagination discovers the latent forces of Nature ... Besides the stars that are established, there is yet another – Imagination – that begets a new star and a new heaven.'

He returned home to Villach in 1524 at the age of thirty-three, to discover that the many cures he had developed had made him famous. When it became known that the great Paracelsus had been appointed town physician and lecturer in medicine at the University of Basel, students flocked to the city from all over Europe, but it was not long before Paracelsus began to antagonise the authorities. On 5 June 1527 he pinned a programme of his forthcoming lectures to the noticeboard of the university, inviting not only students but anyone and everyone. He was compared to Martin Luther (1483–1546), the German leader of the Reformation who, shocked by the wealth and corruption of the papacy, nailed to the chapel door at Wittenberg Castle ninety-five theses attacking the scale of papal indulgences.

Paracelsus wrote, 'Why do men call me a medical Luther? ... I leave it to Luther to defend what he says, and I will be responsible for what I say. That which you wish to Luther, you wish also to me: you wish us both in the fire.' Three weeks later, on 24 June 1527, surrounded by a crowd of cheering students, he burned the books of Avicenna, the Arab 'Prince of Physicians', and those of the Greek physician Galen, in a brass pan with sulphur and nitre in front of the university. The authorities, naturally, were put in mind of Luther burning the papal bull that threatened excommunication only six years earlier.

By the spring of 1528, his contempt for doctors, apothecaries and magistrates made his position completely untenable. His proclamation that his cap had more learning in it than all the heads in the university, and his beard had more experience than all the academies, certainly didn't help. There was a great deal of truth in these undiplomatic statements, however: his introduction of various chemical compounds into medicine resulted in countless 'miraculous' cures that only served further to infuriate the medical establishment, which considered him a 'heretic' and 'usurper'. One of the most efficacious of these cures resulted from Paracelsus' attempt to extract the essential spirit from the poppy. The beneficial effects of the plant had long been known in Europe; however, the alkaloids found in opium are significantly less soluble in water than in alcohol. Paracelsus realised this, and claimed, 'I possess a secret remedy which I call *laudanum* [worthy of praise] and which is superior to all other heroic remedies.' He concocted laudanum by extracting opium into brandy, thus producing, in effect, tincture of morphine. His original brew contained other rather bizarre ingredients such as crushed pearls, henbane, citrus juice and frog-spawn. Paracelsus prescribed his laudanum in the form of three black pills, which he called the Stones of Immortality.

Finally, Paracelsus made so many enemies that he had no choice but to flee for his life in the dead of night. He wandered penniless towards Colmar in Upper Alsace, about fifty miles north of Basel, relying on the hospitality of friends. Over the next eight years he revised old manuscripts and wrote new treatises, including *Der Grossen Wundartzney*, which made his reputation and fortune all over again.

In 1541, Paracelsus was invited to Salzburg by the Prince Palatine Duke Ernest of Bavaria, who was a devotee of the alchemical arts. He died there within six months, on 24 September, in a small room in the White Horse Inn. It is believed by some that he was poisoned or killed in a scuffle by assassins hired by his enemies. He was forty-eight years old.

The first principle of magic, according to Paracelsus, was the extraction of the 'quintessence' from every material object. This rather abstruse notion was drawn from his belief that all objects, whether animal, vegetable or mineral, are possessed of spirit, and that in their totality they are equivalent to the universal spirit or 'astral body' in human beings. This 'astral body' is the essence of the human: the physical body of flesh, blood and bone is merely a container. Paracelsus believed that the human spirit is not indivisible: it is actually composed of smaller and simpler spiritual units to be found in plants and, most importantly, in metals.

According to Paracelsus, the human spirit is the sum of all the lesser spirits contained within the objects of the natural world, just as God is the sum of all the components present within the Universe. It is therefore the goal of the alchemist and wizard to liberate them from the matter to which they are bound, to distil them to purity and unite them with the human body. The occult historian Lewis Spence writes, 'To separate the pure from the impure is, in other words, to seize upon the soul of the heterogeneous bodies – to evolve their "predestined element", "the seminal essence of beings", "the first being, or quintessence".'

The word 'quintessence' is of paramount importance in alchemy, since it refers to the belief that every physical object contains within it four elements, which combine together to form a fifth, which embodies its essential nature, also referred to as its 'mercury'. (This is not the metal mercury known to chemists, but rather the spiritual essence of an object.) Paracelsus himself wrote:

There are as many mercuries as there are things. The mercury of a vegetable, a mineral, or an animal of the same kind, although strongly resembling each other, does not precisely resemble another mercury, and it is for this reason that vegetables, minerals, and animals of the same species are not exactly alike ... The true mercury of philosophers is the radical humidity of each body, and its veritable *semen*, or essence.

Paracelsus sought, within the vegetable kingdom, the analogue of the ultimate purity of gold within the metallic kingdom: a plant that 'should unite in itself the virtues of nearly all the vegetable essences'. In his *Life of Paracelsus*, written at the turn of the nineteenth century, Savarien describes how the great alchemist secured the essence of the plant (it is unclear precisely how he discovered the plant itself):

He [Paracelsus] took some balm-mint in flower, which he had taken care to collect before the rising of the sun. He pounded it in a mortar, reduced it to an impalpable dust, poured it into a long-necked vial, which he sealed hermetically, and placed it to digest (or settle) for forty hours in a heap of horse-dung. This time expired, he opened the vial, and found there a matter which he reduced into a fluid by pressing it, separating it from its impurities by exposure to the slow heat of a *bain-marie*. The grosser parts sank to the bottom, and he drew off the liqueur, which floated on the top, filtering it through some cotton. This liqueur having been poured into a bottle he added it to the fixed salt, which he had drawn from the same plant when dried. There remained nothing more but to extract from this liqueur the first life or being of the plant. For this purpose Paracelsus mixed the liqueur with so much 'water of salt' (understand by this the mercurial element or radical humidity of the salt), put it in a matrass, exposed it for six weeks to the sun, and finally, at the expiration of this term, discovered a last residuum, which was decidedly, according to him, the first life or supreme essence of the plant. But at all events, it is certain that what he found in his matrass was the genie or spirit he required; and with the surplus, if there were any, we need not concern ourselves.

Savarien states that the 'genie' thus obtained by Paracelsus resembled *absinthe*: an emerald-green liquid, which, although very pretty to look at, could by no means be considered the Elixir of Life. Undaunted by this failure, Paracelsus continued with his experiments, extracting the 'predestined elements' from such plants as the gilly-flower, cinnamon, myrrh and the celandine, and incorporating them into his medicinal remedies.

Notwithstanding these experiments with representatives of the vegetable kingdom, Paracelsus's first priority was to isolate the quintessences of metallic life: gold, silver, iron, lead and so on. According to the complex formulae of alchemy, Paracelsus was required to take mercury and sublimate it with sal-ammoniac. He then calcined, coagulated and dissolved it, and strained it for one month until it thickened into a hard substance. The result (which was theoretically achieved following many more secret processes) was a stone able to transform imperfect metals into perfect ones – gold and silver.

Surprisingly, the practice of alchemy did not die out with the development of chemistry in the eighteenth and nineteenth centuries. On the contrary, the alchemists took heart from chemical experiments such as that performed by Lord Rutherford in 1919, in which he successfully transmuted nitrogen into oxygen in the laboratory.

One of those who were most impressed by Rutherford's achievement was a thirty-six-year-old chemical assistant in Munich named Franz Tausend, who had developed his own rather idiosyncratic chemical theories. Tausend wrote a pamphlet entitled *180 Elements, the Atomic Weight, and their Incorporation in the System of Harmonic Periods*, in which he combined Pythagorean theories on the structure of the Universe with the periodic table of elements devised by the Russian chemist Mendeleev in 1863. Tausend believed that every atom in a particular element possessed a certain vibrational frequency, which was related to the atomic weight of the nucleus. He also claimed that this vibrational frequency could be altered, thus transforming one element into another.

In 1924, Tausend's theories came to the attention of General Erich von Ludendorff, who had just been heavily defeated in the German presidential elections by General Hindenburg. Having turned his attention to fund-raising for the Nazis, he was intrigued by rumours that Tausend had succeeded in manufacturing gold, and paid a visit to the chemist in Munich. Five men went with him: Kummer, a chemical engineer; Mannesmann, a successful businessman; a merchant named Stremmel; a banker named Osthoff; and another chemist von Rebay.

With them they took the substances requested by Tausend: iron oxide and quartz. Stremmel instructed Kummer and von Rebay to melt them down, and then took the crucible with him to his hotel room. The next morning, Tausend received them and heated the crucible again in his furnace, adding a small quantity of an unknown white powder. When the contents had been allowed to cool, the crucible was broken open, revealing a seven-gram nugget of gold.

Ludendorff was sufficiently impressed to form a company called Company 164. He would receive 75 per cent of the profits, with 5 per cent going to Tausend. There was no shortage of investors, and of the money that rolled in, Ludendorff diverted 400,000 marks into Nazi Party coffers. The company could not last long with such a drain on its resources, and in December 1926 Ludendorff resigned, leaving Tausend in charge – and liable for the company's considerable debts. In 1929, Tausend was arrested for fraud: no more gold had been produced by the company, although it was rumoured that he had produced 723 grams in a single operation. He was found guilty and imprisoned for four years.

In 1931, a Polish engineer named Dunikovski announced that he had discovered a new form of energy, which he dubbed 'Z rays'. He claimed that this new radiation would transmute common sand or quartz into gold. He convinced investors to put money into his invention, but when he produced no gold, he too was arrested for fraud and imprisoned for four years. However, he was released after two years, thanks to his lawyer, and moved from Paris to San Remo on the Italian Riviera.

It was not long before rumours began to spread that Dunikovski was continuing with his experiments, and selling the occasional nugget of gold. When his lawyer learned of this, he went to visit Dunikovski with the chemist Albert Bonn. They discovered that the sand Dunikovski was using contained a tiny proportion of gold, but were impressed when he proved that with his technique he was able to extract 100 times more gold than with normal methods of extraction.

In 1936, Dunikovski gave a demonstration of his extraction technique to an audience of scientists, and presented his theory that all atoms were in a constant state of transformation, which normally occurred over thousands of years. He called these 'embryonic atoms', and claimed that his process (the details of which he kept to himself) accelerated the growth of embryonic gold in quartz.

In the years following the Second World War, France became the centre of alchemical research. Perhaps the most famous of these modern alchemists was Armand Barbault. In their book *Mysteries of Magic*, Stuart Holroyd and Neil Powell suggest Barbault was inspired by the theory that the name of the Rosicrucians (the secret society of cabbalists, occultists and alchemists) is derived not from *rosa* ('rose' in Latin), but from *ros*, the Latin for 'dew'. According to Holroyd and Powell:

> An essential part of this process ... is the gathering of dew in canvas sheets every morning from March 21 to June 24. The idea of gathering dew was first put forward at the end of the seventeenth century in a mysterious book of

engravings without captions entitled *Mutus Liber*, the *Wordless Book*. The author of another book of about the same date, the *Polygraphice*, writes: 'Gather Dew in the Month of May, with a clean white Linen Cloth spread upon the Grass.' When this filtered dew has been left for fourteen days in horse dung, and then distilled to a quarter of its bulk four times running, it yields a potent Spirit of Dew.' And if you are indeed an Artist you may by this turn all Metals into their first matter.

Barbault's method involves the use of a certain 'germ' found in forest clearings, which is heated steadily in a closed flask, and to which is added dew in which the tips of young plants have been fermented. The final ingredient is something called a 'mother plant'. The temperature is then raised until the contacts of the flask are turned to ash. This ash is then placed in long test tubes along with a small amount of powdered gold. The tubes are partially inserted into an oven at 200°C and the contents boiled. The steam condenses in the upper parts of the tubes, which are outside the oven, and the water trickles down to rehydrate the contents. The result of the process should be a golden liquid, which Barbault regarded as the alchemist's elixir.

It is unlikely that any alchemist ever succeeded in transmuting base metals into gold, or prolonging life indefinitely, or creating artificial, magically endowed creatures. It is certain, however, that many charlatans took advantage of the greedy or gullible with their promises of untold riches. Nevertheless, the Philosopher's Stone remains a tantalising mystery to many students of the occult, who believe that the secret of its creation exists to be discovered one day. And perhaps the day may come when our knowledge of matter and how to control it develops to the point where we can realise the dream of the alchemists through empirical science.

FIVE

The Necromancer

> 'By the mysteries of the deep, by the flames of Banal, by
> the power of the East, and by the silence of the night, by
> the holy rites of Hecate, I conjure and exorcise thee thou
> distressed Spirit, to present thyself here, and reveal unto
> me the cause of thy calamity, why thou didst offer violence
> to thy own liege life, where thou art now in being, and
> where thou wilt hereafter be.'
>
> INVOCATION OF THE SPIRIT OF A SUICIDE,
> FROM REGINALD SCOT, *DISCOVERIE OF WITCHCRAFT*

We now come to what is perhaps the most sinister and disturb-
ing of all the works performed by the wizard: necromancy, or
divination by means of the spirits of the dead. Although derived
from the Greek words *nekros*, dead and *manteia*, divination or
prophecy, it is through its Italian form *nigromancia* that necromancy came to be known as the Black Art. In ancient Greece,
the art of necromancy involved descending into Hades to
consult the dead, as opposed to summoning them into the material world. The oldest known mention of necromancy occurs in
Homer's *Odyssey*, in which Ulysses voyages to Hades and, in
accordance with certain rites described by Circe, evokes the
souls of the dead.

Necromancy is found in every nation in the ancient world,
although its ultimate place of origin is impossible to ascertain
with any certainty. Equally uncertain is the exact nature of the

methods used in the successful practice of the art: as Lewis Spence reminds us, necromancy in the Middle Ages was called sorcery, and yet its ultimate goals are the same as modern Spiritualism. However, it must be said that Spiritualism is a vastly watered-down version of necromancy, which Richard Cavendish describes as one of the ugliest and most dangerous of magical operations. 'It is considered particularly dangerous because the nastiness of its procedures stirs up evil currents and attracts evil forces which may fasten on the magician.'

Necromancy is one of the most important elements in occultism, since it is the raising of souls from the realm of the dead that is the supreme test of the wizard's art. For instance, the necromantic arts were studied in great depth by the great Elizabethan magician, John Dee, whom we shall meet later in this chapter.

No ceremony is necessary if a compact has been made between the magician and the Devil, since a familiar will invariably be present to do its master's bidding. On the other hand, the 'true sorcerer' will prefer to maintain his independence, and to rely on his own knowledge of the occult arts in order to compel the spirits of the dead to appear before him.

The wizard always has an assistant, and together they will prepare the articles necessary for the successful performance of the ritual. Of considerable importance is the place in which the ritual is to be performed; as we noted earlier, the best places tend to be infrequently visited by other people: strange, wild places, such as subterranean caverns or dense woods, or deserts. Empty plains where few travellers venture, and where several roads meet, are also desirable venues for the necromancer's rites, as are the ruins of castles or monasteries, churchyards or seashores.

It is worth noting here that these places are what the anthropologist Victor Turner called 'liminal zones'. They are places of transition, of travel in terms of both space and time. Highways, crossroads, bridges and shores are liminal zones; the hours of dusk and dawn – the boundaries between day and night – are liminal times; so is the turn of the year. It is easy to understand why such locations were (and are) regarded as places where strange things could happen: like the forest, the roads spanning the open country between the safety of habitats were seen as harbouring a host of potential dangers, both natural and supernatural. In these places, the traveller of centuries past kept a wary eye open both for robbers and vampires, sinister vagabonds as well as werewolves. It is an apprehension that has been carried through to contemporary urban life, an apprehension that prompts me, for instance, always to lock the doors when I am travelling by car, day or night. Merely common sense in these violent times? Of course. Just as it was common sense for our ancestors to regard their highways with caution. It may be, as Patrick Harpur states in his fascinating book *Daimonic Reality*, that this is the reason for the high incidence of encounters with all manner of strange beings in liminal zones, where 'the laws of time and space, matter and causality seem attenuated; and we glimpse for an instant an unseen order of things'. Perhaps our heightened sense of our surroundings – the modern versions of predator-haunted forests – at these times forces a subtle alteration in our consciousness, making us more amenable to interaction with hitherto invisible non-human intelligences.

In the place where the necromantic rite is to be performed, it is also desirable for the moon to be shining brightly during the proceedings; alternatively, the weather may be violent in the extreme, with thunder and lightning lashing a sky twisted and tortured by the elements. According to Spence, 'in these places, times, and seasons, it is contended that spirits can with less difficulty manifest themselves to mortal eyes, and continue visible with the least pain, in this elemental external world'.

The wizard and his assistant must prepare themselves very carefully for the perilous undertaking. For nine days prior to the night of the ceremony, they dress themselves in grave-clothes stolen from corpses and, having recited the funeral service over themselves, they partake of a diet of dog's flesh, unsalted and unleavened bread and unfermented grape juice. The dog flesh is consumed because the dog is associated with the fearsome

Hecate, goddess of death and sterility, whose aspect was said to drive humans insane at a single glance. Since salt is a preservative, its absence in the bread signifies putrefaction. Its lack of leaven, and the grape juice's lack of fermentation, symbolise matter without spirit, that which is dead. Cavendish explains that the 'bread and the grape juice are also the necromantic equivalents of the bread and wine of communion, unleavened and unfermented as a sacrament of emptiness and despair'.

The point of these unpleasant activities is to create an occult link between the necromancer and the corpse he intends to raise. Between midnight and one o'clock in the morning he draws a magic circle around the grave. The nature of this circle is, of course, of immense importance. It is drawn within an area nine feet square, at the borders of which parallel lines are drawn containing various occult symbols, such as crosses and triangles. Within this square the first or outer circle is drawn, then, one and a half feet within, the second circle is inscribed. Within this circle, another square is drawn at the centre of which lies the grave of the person to be summoned back to life.

The necromancer then opens the grave, revealing the body within. He touches it three times with his magic wand and commands it to rise. In *The Magical Arts*, Cavendish offers us one example of the formulae that may be used:

> By the virtue of the Holy Resurrection and the agonies of the damned, I conjure and command thee, spirit ... deceased, to answer my demands and obey these sacred ceremonies, on pain of everlasting torment. Berald, Beroald, Balbin, Gab, Gabor, Agaba, arise, arise, I charge and command thee.

When this conjuration has been said, the corpse is taken from its resting place and arranged on the ground with its arms outstretched in a bizarre echo of the crucified Christ, and with its head pointing to the east, the direction of the rising sun. The necromancer then commands the departed spirit to re-enter its body, which slowly rises until it is standing before him. When it has answered the questions put to it, the spirit is allowed to rest: the necromancer destroys the body, either by burning it or placing it in quicklime, so that no one else may call it back to the earth.

Among the most terrifying of necromantic operations are those in which the dead are summoned to attack or enslave the living. Instructions for conducting such horrible rituals are to be found throughout the literature of black magic. The following method comes from ancient Egypt. In order to force a woman to submit to him, the necromancer fashions a wax doll in the image of his target, and then pierces it with thirteen needles, through the brain, eyes, ears, mouth, hands, feet, stomach, anus and genitals. He then goes to the grave of someone who died either violently, or while young, and summons the corpse by invoking the names of Ereshkigal, the Sumerian queen of the underworld; Anubis, the jackal-headed Egyptian god of the dead; and the other gods of the underworld and the spirits who died before their time. The necromancer commands the corpse to leave its grave, go to the woman's house and bring her to him, entreating the corpse not to let her sleep with any other, nor to find sexual pleasure with any other, nor even to be healthy unless she is with the necromancer.

If he wishes to attack an enemy, the necromancer may perform a ceremony connected with Mars, the god of war. He covers his room with scarlet cloth, wears scarlet robes, and uses a sword as his magic wand. His magical equipment also includes a ruby and the astrological symbol of Mars carved upon a steel pentagon. He then invokes the terrible demon Asmodeus, the arch-devil of the fifth Infernal Habitation, and offers himself as the channel through which the demonic force may manifest itself. Of course, in order for the malignant force to be properly directed, a magical link with the target is needed, and this may be a lock of hair, a nail clipping, or perhaps something with which he or she has been in physical contact. If the necromancer has no such object or piece of the target's body, he may forge an artificial link by identifying an item of his own with the target.

There are a number of methods by which this might be done, the most brutal of which is to baptise an animal with the target's name and then torture and kill it; alternatively, the necromancer might take an inanimate object, concentrate all his hatred upon it and then secrete it in the target's house.

It was considered essential that the necromancer possessed formidable powers of concentration, his mind, like a laser beam, a projection of energy to be focused and directed in any direction he chose. As our world is permeated by both good and evil, if the necromancer projected hatred, then that 'beam' would attract evil to itself, and its power was increased dramatically. Concentration could be augmented by conducting what is known as the Black Fast. For instance, abstinence from meat and milk while concentrating one's hatred upon a particular person was believed to cause that person's death.

Of course, such concentration of the magical will could be put to good uses as well as bad (regardless of whether such concentration actually worked). During the Second World War, the British Spiritualist community believed that the Nazis were using (or being used by) monstrous occult powers to further their plans for world domination (see Chapter Eight). They also believed that the only way to stop them would be to use the opposing forces of goodness and light. This the Spiritualists did, paying special attention to British pilots fighting in the Battle of Britain. It is a little-known fact that this additional battle was being waged at the time, with the Spiritualists giving psychic aid to the brave pilots defending the nation's skies. This came to be known as the Magical Battle of Britain.

The Spiritualists were in turn aided in their efforts by the white witches, who feared that a Nazi invasion of Britain was imminent, and would see their extermination. By raising their own occult forces, they hoped to stave off the invasion in the summer of 1940. Travelling to the Kent coast, the witches threw a substance known as 'go-away powder' into the sea. Made according to an ancient recipe, this substance, combined with certain potent magical spells, had the effect (so the witches believed) of raising an impassable psychic barrier around the shores of Britain. Another coven travelled to the Hampshire coast with the intention of raising a magical cone of power that would turn back the advancing forces of Darkness. Indeed, magical operations were carried out by covens all over the country, concentrating on the idea of confusing the minds of Hitler's High Command and making them believe that to invade Britain would be too difficult. In the autumn of 1940, Hitler postponed the invasion of Britain indefinitely.

It was also believed that the necromancer could create an artificial elemental (as opposed to the natural elementals, the mischievous spirits of earth, air, fire and water), by forming in his mind a clear picture of whatever creature he chose for the task. He concentrates all his hatred and willpower on the mental image until it becomes possessed of its own temporary life. It can then be sent out to attack the necromancer's enemy. The only people who will be able to see this creature are those who are clairvoyant, and the victim himself or herself. There are a number of ways in which a person may know that he or she is the victim of a psychic attack of this kind. They may feel unaccountably afraid, or may discover inexplicable bruises on the body. They may find smears of slime in their homes, which may contain strange footprints; they may detect the odour of rotting flesh; or there may be unexplained fires or loud noises in the house.

All of the above assumes that the necromantic operation has proceeded according to plan. However, if something goes wrong, or if the magician makes a mistake in the ritual, the attack can rebound upon him. The magician may be alerted to this by experiencing terrifying nightmares in which he sees strange and evil beings; dreadful smells around the house; or inexplicable pools of blood. Cavendish offers the example of Eliphas Levi, the great French occultist, who claimed that sometimes, after performing a ritual, his sleep was disturbed by the sensation of a hand around his throat. He would find his books and papers were scattered around the room, and he would hear heavy blows thundering on the ceiling.

Necromancy was not always concerned with raising the dead. Demons, too, could be summoned by the skilled necromancer, although this operation was even more dangerous. In his *Autobiography*, the famous Italian sculptor Benvenuto Cellini (1500–71) relates a fascinating anecdote regarding an incident that happened in Rome in 1534. He claims to have made the acquaintance of a Sicilian priest, a man of considerable learning who was well versed in Greek and Latin. One day, the two men were having a conversation about the art of necromancy. Cellini had always been fascinated by the subject, and asked the priest if he knew anything of this dark, dangerous and mysterious art.

The priest grew suddenly serious, and replied that any man who entered into a study of necromancy had to be of very sound and stable mind indeed. Cellini declared that he was such a man: he had the courage, presence of mind and emotional stability to withstand the shock of any information his friend might care to present him with. The priest considered this for some moments, and presently replied that, if Cellini thought he was up to the venture, then he would satisfy his curiosity. Thus, wrote Cellini, they agreed to enter upon a scheme of necromancy.

The priest instructed Cellini to look for a companion or two to participate with them in the experiment. Cellini invited a close friend named Vincenzio Romoli, who in turn invited another, unnamed man, who was from the town of Pistoia and who was himself an experienced necromancer. The three men went to the Coliseum, and the priest, according to the custom practised by necromancers, began to draw a magic circle upon the ground, and to make a fire. He had brought with him all manner of arcane substances, some of which exuded wonderful fragrances, while others emitted the unholiest of stenches.

When he had completed his occult preparations, the priest made an opening in the circle, and led his companions into the centre. He then instructed the necromancer from Pistoia to cast certain perfumes into the fire at specific times, while he himself began the complex incantations designed to raise the dead.

The ceremony lasted more than an hour and a half, and when

it was complete (so Cellini claims) the Coliseum was filled with legions of devils that cavorted through the great amphitheatre. The priest turned to Cellini, and told him to ask them something. Cellini thought for a moment, and then cried out to them that he required them to bring him into company with his Sicilian mistress, Angelica. Although the demons declined to grant his request, nevertheless Cellini was deeply impressed with this demonstration of the necromantic art.

The priest told Cellini that they should make a second attempt, and that this time he would be satisfied in whatever he asked. He added that Cellini should bring with him a boy who had never known a night with a woman. Cellini decided to take his apprentice, who was twelve years old. Vincenzio Romoli also accompanied them again, together with a man named Agnolino Gaddi, another of Cellini's close friends.

They arrived at the Coliseum to find that the priest had already performed the preparations for the ritual; and Cellini noticed that the circle he had drawn was more elaborate, and had been drawn with greater care, than on the previous occasion. Having instructed Romoli and Gaddi to sprinkle the requisite perfumes upon the fire at the correct times, the priest then gave Cellini a magical chart, or *pintacolo*, and instructed him to hold it aloft in the direction of the young apprentice.

Then, in a loud and terrifying voice, the priest called forth a multitude of demons by their names. These demons were the commanders of the legions that had appeared on the previous occasion. By the power of the eternal and uncreated God, who lives for ever in the languages of the Holy Land, in Greek and in Latin, the priest commanded the infernal leaders to bring forth their minions. Immediately the amphitheatre was once again filled with demons, a hundred times greater in number than at the previous ceremony.

As his friends continued to pay attention to the fire and the perfumes, Cellini once again cried out to the demons that he wished to be in the company of his mistress, Angelica. The priest turned to him and declared that the demons assured him that he would be with her in the space of one month. He then told Cellini to stand beside him, and not to falter from his position, because there were now a thousand more demons in the amphitheatre than he had intended. In addition, they were also the most powerful and dangerous of fiends, and in view of the fact that they had answered Cellini's question, it was in their best interests for the priest to entreat them politely to be on their way.

Cellini's young apprentice had by this time become paralysed with terror, and was screaming that the place was filled with a million fearsome men who wanted to slaughter them, and that there were also four enormous giants who were attempting to break into their protective magic circle.

The priest himself was becoming increasingly alarmed and afraid, and continued to entreat the demons to depart peacefully. Romoli, who was quivering like a leaf, continued his ministrations over the fire, while Cellini himself did his best to stand firm beside the priest, although in truth he was just as petrified as the rest of them. But when he glanced across at the priest, and saw the look of absolute and hopeless terror on the man's face, he gave himself up for dead.

The boy leaned forward and placed his head between his knees, saying that this was the attitude in which he would die, for he had no doubt that death would claim them all this night. Cellini told him to take courage: the demons, he said, were still under their control and were nothing but smoke and shadow. He ordered the boy to raise up his head and face down his terror. As soon as the boy looked up, he screamed that the amphitheatre was on fire, and that they would all be consumed. Covering his eyes with shaking hands, he cried that this was surely the end of them, and he had no wish to see more.

Cellini turned to Romoli and instructed him to burn the most precious of the magical perfumes, and then turned towards Gaddi, who was half dead with terror. He shouted at him to pull himself together, and to help Romoli with the perfumes. Gaddi attempted to move, but when he did so the result was, according to Cellini, annoying both to their sense of hearing and smell, and overcame the perfumes.

In spite of their predicament, Cellini could not help but burst out laughing at this. When he heard the laughter, the boy raised his head once again, and declared in surprise and wonder that the demons were flying away. The companions all stayed exactly where they were, not daring to move a muscle until the bell rang for morning prayers. The boy cried out again that now there were very few devils left, and they were very far away. The priest performed the concluding ceremonies of the necromantic ritual, and the companions left the magic circle, trembling with relief and exhaustion.

As they were returning to their houses in the district of Banchi, the boy told them that he could see two of the demons leaping and skipping across the rooftops ahead of them. The priest declared that he had performed magical operations many times, but never had he had such an astonishing adventure. As they continued on their way, he asked Cellini if he would be interested in collaborating on a book, which, he declared, would certainly make them a fortune. He then suggested that they summon the demons again, and ask them to divulge the location of the world's treasures. Perhaps, he continued, they should also ask which love affairs would bring them happiness, and which would be a waste of time.

But it seems that Cellini did not participate further in such experiments.

There have been countless magicians through the ages who have practised the art of necromancy. By far the most famous of these is the Elizabethan magus Dr John Dee, whose magical legacy lives on in the arcane world of the occult.

John Dee was born in London on 13 July 1527. His father was a vintner, who also held a minor position in the court of Henry VIII. Since his family enjoyed a reasonable level of affluence, Dee received a good education, going to Cambridge at the age of fifteen and taking his BA degree two years later. Possessed of a powerful and endlessly enquiring mind, Dee decided to leave England for a while and study abroad. In 1547 he went to the Netherlands, where he met with a number of scholars, who cultivated his growing interest in astronomy.

He then travelled on to France, arriving in Paris in 1550. Following a number of lectures he delivered on the principles of geometry, Dee was offered a permanent position at the Sorbonne. However, he declined, preferring to return to England, where Edward VI granted him the rectory of Upton-on-Severn in Worcestershire.

Dee now found himself in a splendid position, with a regular income, a comfortable home and plenty of time to pursue his own interests. Unfortunately, his life quickly took a turn for the worse, when in 1553 he was accused of trying to kill the newly crowned Queen Mary through occult means. Following a brief imprisonment at Hampton Court, he noted that many people now viewed him with considerable mistrust. He wrote with considerable irritation in his preface to an English translation of Euclid that he was considered 'a companion of the hellhounds, a caller and a conjurer of wicked and damned spirits'.

Fortunately for Dee, this situation was not to last; and with the reign of Elizabeth I he found his circumstances rapidly improving. Following another trip abroad, he took up residence at Mortlake on the Thames, where his fame as an astronomer of renown quickly spread.

Dee's life took a new direction following his experiments in crystallomancy, or divination by means of crystals. At this time he was living a rather solitary life, practising astrology for a living and studying alchemy in his spare time. He constantly used one of the archetypal wizard's accoutrements, the crystal ball, into which he would gaze for long hours, hoping that it might afford him some glimpse of the arcane workings of the Universe. On 25 May 1581, he saw spirits for the first time, moving through the glinting substance of the magical globe.

In November of the following year, he experienced a more profound event. While on his knees praying in his laboratory,

Dee became aware of a vastly powerful and divine presence. Looking towards the west window, he saw an intensely bright light, in the midst of which stood the angel Uriel. Dee tried to speak, but was struck dumb with awe at the incredible sight.

The angel looked down upon the human being with love, and offered him a gentle smile, as if to reassure him that he had nothing to fear. Then, holding out an object that appeared to be a convex crystal, the celestial being told Dee that this was a means by which he would be able to communicate with the beings of other worlds. All he had to do was gaze into it, and spirits would immediately appear and converse with him, revealing the mysteries of the Universe and telling him of future events. With that, Uriel vanished.

Without delay, Dee began to experiment with the strange celestial artefact, looking into its depths and finding (to his surprise) that it took the utmost concentration before the spirits could be persuaded to appear before him. Although his experiments ultimately seemed to be successful, with much discourse flowing between him and the spirits who came to him through the celestial crystal, Dee could never remember the nature of that discourse. It seemed that forgetfulness was the price he was required to pay for communion with the other world. The price was, of course, too high for Dee, for what use was the information if one immediately forgot it?

He therefore set himself the task of finding an assistant, a scryer, who would be able to converse with the spirits while Dee wrote down the dialogue. He chose a man by the name of Barnabas Saul, who apparently had some success in contacting spirits to begin with, until he experienced a troubling encounter with some kind of 'spiritual creature' one night. Following this, Saul's talents seem to have diminished, until finally he informed Dee that he was unable to see anything within the celestial crystal. Disappointed, Dee dismissed him and resumed his search for a useful assistant.

Dee finally found the man he thought he was looking for in the person of Edward Kelly, a native of Lancashire born in 1555.

Kelly always wore a black skull-cap, which lent him an air of occult mystery, although it represented an altogether more mundane and tawdry past. At Lancaster he had been convicted of coining, the practice by which the edges of coins were shaved off imperceptibly, and the fragments melted down to produce new coins. Kelly suffered the penalty for this crime: the tops of his ears were cut off – a 'coining' of an altogether more painful sort. Kelly was a charlatan who pursued his dreams of wealth and luxury through any means necessary, legal or otherwise. Having made a study of magic and alchemy (thus acquiring a reputation as a necromancer and alchemist), he had taken to preying upon the greedy and gullible, relieving them of their money while promising to secure them untold wealth by means of the Philosopher's Stone, which he claimed to have discovered.

Spence offers a gruesome anecdote in which Kelly took a wealthy client and some of his servants into the park of Walton le Dale near Preston, Lancashire one night, and 'there alarmed him with the most terrific incantations'. Kelly then asked one of his client's servants which body had most recently been buried in the neighbouring churchyard. When the servant replied that a man had been laid to rest only a few hours previously, Kelly demanded to be taken to the fellow's grave. He proceeded to exhume the corpse and then pretended to converse with it, claiming that it was providing him with information on future events.

Kelly was altogether more useful as an assistant to Dee than Barnabas Saul had been: for one thing, he had a much more vivid imagination, with which he did not hesitate to impress his new employer. As soon as he was set to work gazing into the celestial crystal, he feigned awe and wonder, providing Dee with amazing (and completely fabricated) information and insights regarding the world of the spirits to which the crystal gave him access. Dee was overjoyed. At last, he believed, he had found an able scryer who would be able to act as a channel between this world and those of the spirits. Although Dee possessed a powerful and penetrating intellect, Kelly was an equally accomplished confidence trickster who had no qualms about taking full advantage of his master's passionate search for truth.

On many occasions, Kelly would cleverly pique Dee's curiosity further by becoming frightened at what he experienced while using the celestial crystal. He would wonder aloud whether the work upon which they were engaged was entirely free from danger, and would claim to have seen terrible, unholy things within the crystal, which were not of Heaven, horrible demons reaching up from the depths of Hell to destroy them. All this Dee faithfully recorded, and the material was eventually published in 1659 under the title *A True and Faithful Relation of what passed between Dr John Dee and some spirits; tending, had it succeeded, to a General Alteration of most States and Kingdoms in the World.*

Dee's method of communicating with the realm of spirits utilised a table containing one of several charts consisting of forty-nine by forty-nine squares, each of which contained a letter. Kelly would sit close by at what they called the Holy Table, on which lay a corresponding chart of numbered squares, and gaze into the celestial crystal until he spied the figure of an angel. Using a wand, the angel would indicate the letters of the message it wished to impart. Kelly then called out these numbers to Dee, who wrote down the letter in the corresponding square.

The messages were in the language of Enochian, which Dee claimed to have received from an angel, and which was the language spoken in Heaven. The *Book of Enoch* is an Apocryphal book of the Old Testament, written (in Hebrew) about a century before Christ. Only fragments of it remained until the traveller Bruce brought back a copy from Abyssinia in 1773. The book describes the spiritual world in great detail, and also Sheol, the place of wickedness. It contains a history of the fallen angels, how they had intercourse with the daughters of men, and the foundation of magic. According to the Book of Enoch:

[In] those days the sons of men having multiplied, there were born to them daughters of great beauty. And when the angels, or sons of heaven, beheld them, they were filled with desire; wherefore they said to one another: 'Come let us choose wives from among the race of man, and let us beget children.' Their leader Samyasa answered thereupon and said: 'Perchance you will be wanting in the courage needed to fulfil this resolution, and then I alone shall be answerable for your fall.' But they swore that they would in no wise repent and that they would achieve their whole design. Now there were two hundred who descended on Mount Armon, and it was from this time that the mountain received its designation, which signifies Mount of the Oath. Hereinafter follow the names of those angelic leaders who descended with this object: Samyasa, chief among all, Urakabarameel, Azibeel, Tamiel, Ramuel, Danel, Azkeel, Sarakuyal, Asael, Armers, Batraal, Anane, Zavebe, Sameveel, Ertrael, Turel, Jomiael, Arizial. They took wives with whom they had intercourse, to whom they also taught Magic, the art of enchantment and the diverse properties of roots and trees. Amazarac gave instruction in all secrets of sorcerers; Barkaial was the master of those who study the stars; Akibeel manifested signs; and Azaradel taught the motions of the moon.

The unlawful revelation of the secrets of Heaven by these rebellious angels upset the harmony between the human and divine, and it took the Deluge to wipe out the profanity and restore balance.

The angels who communicated with Dee claimed that their language was that of the angels of the *Book of Enoch*. The curious thing about Enochian is that it possesses grammar and syntax, just as genuine languages do. It is of course possible that Kelly invented Enochian as a means to further convince Dee of his mediumistic abilities; but, as Colin Wilson notes, this assumption presents difficulties. 'The basic Enochian texts amount to nineteen "keys" [magical invocations], the longest being about 300 words; most amount to about 100. *A Dictionary of Enochian* compiled by Leo Vinci contains about 900 words.' If Kelly invented the celestial language, he would have had to translate the invocations into consistent Enochian and then memorise them all. We must consider, in addition, the method by which the messages from the spirits were transmitted, with Kelly telling Dee which row and column of the chart the spirit indicated. Kelly would thus have needed to know by heart the positions of all the letters and symbols on all the charts. As if this were not a sufficiently great feat of memory for Kelly to perform, all the messages from the spirits were transmitted backwards, since to pronounce the Enochian words forwards would release forces with which Dee and Kelly would not be able to cope.

That Enochian is a complex and consistent language has long been established, and therefore it is regarded by many as the most impressive evidence for the existence of non-human intelligences. Its effectiveness in magical operations has also been attested by many practitioners.

This curious occult partnership quickly became famous throughout England and continental Europe, yet more so when Dee claimed to have discovered the Elixir of Life among the ruins of Glastonbury Abbey. When Albert Laski, Count Palatine of Siradz, visited Elizabeth's court, the Queen placed him in the care of the Earl of Leicester, who took him on a tour of England's finest sights, including her two great universities. Although greatly impressed with what he had been shown, the Count nevertheless informed Leicester of his profound disappointment at not having met Dr Dee.

A few days later, Leicester was waiting with the Polish nobleman for an audience with Elizabeth, when the Earl spied Dee from the Queen's antechamber, and introduced the two men. Dee and Laski got along very well, and the Count paid many visits to Dee's house at Mortlake. Their growing friendship did not escape the attention of the wily Kelly, who noted Laski's belief in the occult and supernatural with satisfaction. Here, he decided, was a new potential source of money. Almost immediately, in Kelly's hands the celestial crystal began to provide them with tantalising hints of an illustrious future for Laski (who naturally paid Dee and Kelly handsomely for their services), the spirits apparently having become fascinated with European politics. Dee was as fascinated with the spirits' pronouncements as Laski. Spence notes:

> It is impossible to come to any other conclusion than that he [Dee] was imposed upon by Kelly, and accepted his revelations as the actual utterances of the spirits; and it seems probable that the clever, plastic, slippery Kelly not only knew something of the optical delusions then practised by the pretended necromancers, but possessed considerable ventriloquial powers, which largely assisted in his nefarious deceptions.

Kelly had begun to entertain curious and self-aggrandising notions of bringing about a seismic shift in the power politics of Europe, with Laski occupying centre stage in a new monarchy and he, Kelly, sitting at his right hand. The spirits, of course, were not slow in providing divine confirmation of these momentous future events: at one point an angel named Murifre came through via the celestial crystal to claim that Laski was destined 'to effect the regeneration of the world'.

Kelly was playing Dee and Laski with the consummate skill of the virtuoso conman, returning to his earlier strategy of becoming frightened at the potential dangers of communicating with transhuman spirits. He threatened to stop scrying, which had the intended effect of throwing both Dee and Laski into panic at the thought of losing such a talented communicator with the astral world.

Kelly then claimed that he had to go to Islington on some business, and Dee became worried that this might be a pretext for leaving Mortlake permanently. In his *Diary* Dee writes:

> ... I asked him why he so hasted to ride thither, and I said if it were to ride to Mr Harry Lee I would go thither, and

to be acquainted with him, seeing now I had so good leisure, being eased of the book writing. Then he said that one told him the other day that the duke [Laski] did but flatter him, and told him other things both against the duke and me. I answered for the duke and myself, and also said that if the forty pounds annuity which Mr Lee did offer him was the chief cause of his mind setting that way (contrary to many of his former promises to me), that then I would assure him of fifty pounds yearly, and would do my best, by following of my suit, to bring it to pass as soon as I possibly could; and thereupon did make him promise upon the Bible.

Then Edward Kelly again upon the same Bible did swear unto me constant friendship, and never to forsake me; and moreover said that unless this had so fallen about he would have gone beyond the seas, taking ship at Newcastle within eight days next.

And so we plight our faith each to the other, taking each other by the hand, upon these points of brotherly and friendly fidelity during life, which covenant I beseech God to turn to his honour, glory, and service, and the comfort of our brethren (his children) here on earth.

The matter of Kelly's payment resolved, he put aside his fears regarding conversing with spirits and returned to scrying with the celestial crystal, informing Laski that he was destined to win glorious victories over the Saracens. However, Kelly added, it would be necessary for the duke to return to Poland, and to take Dee, Kelly, their wives and families with him, to which Laski readily agreed.

The journey took several weeks, and by modern standards the travellers could be said to have gone First Class, at Laski's expense, of course. They arrived at Laski's main estate, Lasco, in early February 1584, and Dee and Kelly immediately began work on the alchemical transmutation of lead into gold, for the purposes of financing the regeneration of Europe predicted by the spirits. Although Laski supplied them with everything they would need, they always seemed to fail just when it looked as if transmutation was about to occur. So close, and yet so far ...

The great alchemical work continued for months, financed by Laski, who was obliged to mortgage estate after estate, until it became obvious to both Dee and Kelly that the duke's fortune was all but exhausted. Kelly consulted the spirits, who of course had been watching events with great interest, and who confided in him that they were now uncertain whether Laski was, after all, the right choice for Europe's great new regenerative monarch. Kelly begged the spirits to reconsider their choice of Laski to be the new leader of Europe, but they were unswerving in their conviction that he was not the man for the job.

At this point, Laski himself began to realise that he was being taken for a very expensive ride, and decided that it would be a very good thing for Dee and Kelly to leave as soon as possible. He suggested to them that they should travel to Prague; he would provide them with the funds for the journey, and also with letters of introduction to the Emperor Rudolph. Astonishingly, Kelly almost immediately received a communication from the spirits instructing Dee to go to Prague and deliver a message from them to the emperor! Marvelling at such a coincidence, the two accepted Laski's suggestion.

Dee and Kelly were welcomed with open arms by the emperor, who was most gratified to make the acquaintance of such a famous philosopher as the renowned Dr Dee, though he was immediately suspicious of Kelly. Although they lived well for a time on the funds given to them by Laski, they were forced to flee Prague in May 1586 following a papal order to imprison and burn heretical magicians. There followed a period of wanderings in which Dee and Kelly eked out a rather meagre existence telling fortunes. After a brief association with Stephen, King of Poland, who quickly grew tired of their constant requests for money, they found a new dupe in the person of Count Rosenberg, a Bohemian nobleman who possessed a number of large estates in

Trebona. They remained at Rosenberg's castle for the next two years, continuing their alchemical experiments, but still failing to gain the ultimate prize of the Philosopher's Stone.

Dee's and Kelly's relationship began to undergo considerable strain. Kelly felt himself to be completely in control of the brilliant but credulous Dee, and yet it was Dee who was famous, and who received the respect and admiration of the many scholars they visited. They quarrelled frequently, and matters were not helped by the desire Kelly had begun to cultivate for Dee's beautiful wife.

Becoming more and more obsessed with possessing the handsome young woman, Kelly at last hit upon a solution. Following yet another threat to resign his position as Dee's scryer, Kelly suggested they consult the spirits. When the session was over, Kelly feigned surprise and horror at what the spirits had said to him, and refused to repeat it to Dee. However, Dee was deeply intrigued and ordered Kelly to tell him what had been said. As if under great emotional stress, Kelly finally blurted out that the spirits had instructed them to exchange wives. Dee was thunderstruck, and Kelly was careful to display his utter abhorrence of the suggestion. The spirits, he claimed, had stated that this was an order from God, and an order from God could not be a sin. He added finally that this was proof that the spirits were not denizens of Heaven, but of the infernal regions, and with that he left the castle.

His invaluable scryer gone, Dee attempted to train his own son Arthur in the art of crystal gazing; but the youth was too lacking in imagination (and too honest) to take Kelly's place. Dee now despaired of finding a scryer with the incredible abilities of Kelly. Of course, Kelly was not long absent: he presently returned to the castle and offered to ask the spirits once again if it was absolutely necessary for him and Dee to swap wives. They replied that it most certainly was, that it would in effect represent their understanding of God's law that all property should be shared equally among humanity. Dee, however, was too overjoyed at the return of his colleague to argue, although their wives, when informed of the spirits' instructions, argued mightily for some time.

Eventually, however, they succumbed to the 'will of God', and Dee wrote that 'on Sunday the 3rd of May, *anno* 1587 ... I, John Dee, Edward Kelly, and our two wives covenanted with God, and subscribed the same for indissoluble and inviolable unities, charity, and friendship keeping, between us four, and all things between us to be common, as God by sundry means willed us to do'.

As might be expected, this new arrangement (which remained less than satisfactory for the women) caused increasing strife among Dee, Kelly and their wives, who began to quarrel furiously with each other. Their financial problems returned with a vengeance, and Dee began to think with nostalgia of his home in England. He received permission from Elizabeth to return, and finally parted company with Kelly, who left for Prague.

Whatever schemes he may have had for relieving the gullible of their money were put to flight when he was arrested upon his arrival by order of the emperor. Released from prison a few months later, Kelly wandered through Germany, telling fortunes and perpetrating the odd magical confidence trick when the opportunity presented itself.

It was not long before he was arrested again on charges of heresy and sorcery. He attempted to escape from his cell by twisting his bedclothes into a rope, but fell from the wall and broke both his legs. He died from his injuries shortly afterwards, in February 1593.

Dee departed for England in 1588. Once again he was penniless, and his friends managed to raise about £500 for him. Back in Mortlake, he again devoted himself to alchemical studies, employing two scryers, Bartholomew and Heckman, to gaze into the celestial crystal. Like Kelly, the two were charlatans, but they lacked his flair for outrageous invention, and were unable to supply him with any useful information from the other world.

In abject poverty he begged the queen for help, and she was prevailed upon to grant him a pension of £200, although he never received it. Eventually he obtained an appointment as Chancellor of St Paul's Cathedral, and in 1595 he exchanged this for the wardenship of Manchester College. About 1602 or 1603, age and intellectual decline forced him to retire, and he returned to his home at Mortlake to try to make ends meet by practising as a fortune teller, 'gaining little in return but the unenviable reputation of a wizard', as Spence has it. Dee died destitute in December 1608.

Dee was unfortunate in his association with the charlatan Edward Kelly; although he practised the necromantic arts, and in so doing exposed himself to potential danger, he was nevertheless a sincere seeker after both spiritual and scientific truths. The world of occultism, however, is full of people like Kelly. Just as the netherworld is said to be inhabited by liars and spiritual confidence tricksters, so is this world home to those who will jump at any chance to hoodwink the gullible and relieve them of their money. Kelly was one; Cagliostro was another, and it is to his life that we now turn.

SIX

The Eighteenth-Century Rake

'He was probably a little mad.'

LEWIS SPENCE, *ENCYCLOPAEDIA OF OCCULTISM*

In one respect, the history of wizardry is like that of any other human endeavour: occasionally there appears a figure that achieves true greatness, and a fame that transcends his life and work. One such man was Apollonius of Tyana; another was Count Alessandro Cagliostro, although Cagliostro has achieved fame more for his clever trickery than his desire to shape the spiritual development of humanity. Although not quite a prize physical specimen (he was small in stature with a dark complexion, a fat body, round head and stiff neck), he was, in modern parlance, a 'superstar' of magic and the occult, and his charisma and enigmatic nature still have the power to enchant and captivate the imagination today. He is, nevertheless, a highly ambivalent figure, and during his lifetime inspired strong opinions and feelings both for him and against. In the nineteenth century his reputation especially suffered at the hands of no less a figure than Thomas Carlyle, who called him the 'Prince of Quacks'. Later historians, notably W. R. H. Trowbridge, came to reassess his life, suggesting that, while he was certainly very far from being an upstanding citizen, he may not have been quite the out-and-out charlatan Carlyle would have us believe.

In addition, it is certainly true that he was and is an extremely controversial figure in occult circles. Lewis Spence called him 'one of the greatest occult figures of all time', and it seems that his true nature lay somewhere between this and Carlyle's altogether less sympathetic view. The British writer on the supernatural Peter Underwood stated that 'while he seems to have been party to a number of disgraceful intrigues and forgeries, he was nevertheless a true wizard'.

Cagliostro was probably born Giuseppe Balsamo (there is much difference of opinion even as to this apparently straightforward piece of information) in 1743 in Sicily. His father, Peter Balsamo, died when Cagliostro was young and his mother, unable to support him, looked to her brother for assistance. Although her brother attempted to help with his upbringing, the boy proved all but unmanageable, demonstrating little interest in formal education, and absconding several times from the religious seminary at Palermo in which he was placed. He was sent next to a Benedictine convent where the Father Superior discovered the boy's natural aptitude for chemistry, and arranged for him to become the assistant of an apothecary attached to the convent. Here he received a reasonably thorough grounding in the principles of chemistry and medicine, although he was invariably more interested in pursuing his own researches than in paying attention to his teacher.

It was not long before he grew bored with his life in the convent, and so once again he escaped and made straight for Palermo, finding a new home among the criminal fraternity there. He is said to have been involved in crimes too numerous to mention, including murder. He was just fourteen years old at the time. Later, as Spence has it, 'becoming tired of lesser villainies he resolved upon a grand stroke, upon which to lay the foundations of his fortunes'.

Cagliostro, then seventeen, chose for his dupe a stupid, greedy and superstitious goldsmith named Marano. Posing as an expert on the occult, alchemy and the supernatural, Cagliostro cultivated a friendship with Marano, who believed strongly in the power and efficacy of magic. Marano bemoaned the fact that he had wasted a great deal of money on charlatans who boasted alchemical knowledge, but had not made good on their claims. In spite of this, he said, he believed that in Cagliostro he had discovered a true master of the occult arts. The latter responded by letting him in on a great secret: in a field near Palermo there lay a considerable treasure, which Cagliostro would be able to find with the aid of certain magical ceremonies.

There was a catch, however: in order to perform these ceremonies, Cagliostro would need certain items, including 60 ounces of gold, representing a small fortune even today, let alone in the mid-eighteenth century. Marano said this would not be possible, to which Cagliostro blithely replied that he would therefore be obliged to enjoy the treasure alone. This had precisely the desired effect on the greedy and avaricious goldsmith, who eventually agreed to supply Cagliostro with everything he needed for the ceremony.

They entered the field at midnight, and Cagliostro began his bogus incantations while Marano, convinced that infernal powers were about to manifest, threw himself on the ground in terror. At that moment, Cagliostro's accomplices appeared, a group of violent thugs who beat Marano mercilessly before stealing his gold. News of this crime quickly spread through Palermo, and Cagliostro was obliged to vacate the city immediately. He made for Messina, where he decided to adopt the undeserved title of 'Count'.

Some time after his arrival in Messina, while out walking around the harbour, the next chapter in Cagliostro's colourful life began. He encountered there an enigmatic character who was dressed in the manner of an Oriental, with caftan and robes, and who had with him an Albanian greyhound. Struck by his unusual appearance, Cagliostro introduced himself. The man, who appeared to be about fifty years old, responded politely and offered to tell Cagliostro the story of his highly eventful life. The stranger pointed out his house, and invited Cagliostro to visit him just before midnight, and to knock twice and then three times more slowly, whereupon he would be admitted.

That night, Cagliostro did as he was bidden, and was led into a narrow, dimly lit passage, at the end of which was a large, candle-lit room containing numerous items of alchemical equipment. The host, who had introduced himself as Althotas, made Cagliostro welcome, and discussed his theories of magic. According to Spence, Althotas 'expressed himself as a believer in the mutability of physical law rather than of magic, which he regarded as a science having fixed laws discoverable and reducible to reason'. He informed his young guest that he was planning to travel to Egypt, and wondered if Cagliostro would consider accompanying him. Cagliostro readily agreed.

Althotas said that he had no money with him, but that this would not be a problem, since he possessed the secret of manufacturing gold. He also said that he was far older than he looked, possessing as he did another secret: that of preserving youth.

The two bought passage on a Genoese ship bound for Alexandria, and during this voyage Althotas volunteered a little information about himself. He claimed to know nothing of his place of birth or his parents, adding that he had spent his early years near Tunis, where he had been the slave of a wealthy Muslim pirate. At twelve he was fluent in Arabic, studied botany and read the Koran to his master, who died when Althotas was sixteen.

Following their travels through Egypt, they travelled south and east, visiting kingdoms throughout Africa and Asia, finally establishing a base on Rhodes, where they pursued their alchemical researches. From there they travelled to Malta, where Althotas seems to have died (at any rate, he makes no further appearance in the life of Cagliostro).

Following Althotas' death, Cagliostro travelled to Naples, where he became acquainted with a Sicilian prince who so enjoyed his company that he invited Cagliostro to his castle near Palermo. He was taking his life in his hands by returning to the haunts of his youth, where he had committed so many crimes, few of which had been forgotten. On a trip to Messina, he ran into one of his old friends, one of the thugs who had turned over the goldsmith, Marano. His friend told him that it was indeed dangerous for him to stay in Messina, or even to return to Palermo, and suggested that Cagliostro join him in a little venture he was planning, to open a casino in Naples in which wealthy foreigners might be relieved of their cash.

The casino was a success, so much so that it attracted the attention of the Neapolitan authorities who took a dim view of their activities. It was time to move on again, this time to the Papal States. Accounts of Cagliostro's life offer few details as to how he passed his time here, aside from confirming that he parted company with his colleague, and continued to prey on the naïve and stupid.

Not long after, he seems to have established himself as an apothecary in Rome, offering remedies for all manner of ailments and making a great deal of money. It was here in Rome that he met a beautiful young woman named Lorenza Feliciani with whom he immediately fell in love and proposed marriage. Her father's consent was a mere formality, such was Cagliostro's apparent wealth. Lorenza was, by all accounts, a delightful young woman, charming, honest, endearingly modest and completely devoted to her new husband.

Cagliostro's biographers are unanimous in their opinion that her marriage to Cagliostro signalled the beginning of Lorenza's moral decline. While it is certainly true that his shady character made him a less than suitable match for her, the exact nature of their relationship is open to debate. Lewis Spence writes:

> The most dreadful accusations have been made concerning the manner in which Cagliostro treated his wife, and it has been alleged that he thoroughly ruined her character and corrupted her mind. But ... this account has been coloured by the unscrupulous imagination of the Jesuitical writers of the Roman Inquisition. All biographers agree that Cagliostro hastened his wife's ruin, but it is difficult to

know how they came by their data; and in any case they disagree substantially in their details.

It is agreed by all, however, that the couple's household quickly became the headquarters of various conmen and other ne'er-do-wells. Following a disagreement with certain of these villains, Cagliostro and Lorenza were forced to flee Rome in the company of a character called the Marquis D'Agriata. They headed for Venice, and stopped in the town of Bergamo, which they were again compelled to leave hastily following more scams perpetrated upon the unsuspecting population. For the next few years they wandered through Southern Europe, finally ending up in Barcelona. They stayed there for six months before moving on to Madrid and then Lisbon. They then set sail for England and moved into an apartment in Whitcomb Street, London, where Cagliostro continued to dupe foreigners while also continuing his studies in chemistry and physics.

In 1772 Cagliostro and Lorenza left for France, taking with them an acquaintance named Duplaisir. Soon after their arrival, Duplaisir eloped with Lorenza. Cagliostro pursued them and had his wife arrested. She spent several months in a penitentiary; however, it is said that upon her release, she and Cagliostro were immediately reconciled.

It seems that Cagliostro's alchemical researches met with some success in France, which drew him to the attention of Parisian society. Such was the taste for mysticism in Europe at the time that he became a great favourite among the aristocracy. Nevertheless, once again he went too far with his claims, and the resulting suspicions that were harboured against him forced him to flee with Lorenza, first to Brussels, and then back to Palermo.

News of his return to his native town spread quickly, and reached the ears of the goldsmith Marano, who promptly had him arrested. Luck, however, was once again on Cagliostro's side. A Sicilian nobleman stepped in and arranged for Cagliostro's release and, with Lorenza, he recommended his meandering travels, first to Malta, then Naples, Marseilles and

Barcelona. It was in this city that Cagliostro cheated a certain alchemist of 100,000 crowns and so, yet again, the couple had to flee, this time back to England.

In London, Cagliostro became a Mason, having seen the potential financial benefits of membership. He set about visiting the various London Lodges, making friends among their rich and powerful members. While browsing in a bookstall one day, Cagliostro came across an odd manuscript, which apparently had belonged to one George Gaston, about whom nothing is known. The manuscript was essentially a treatise on Egyptian Masonry, and contained a great deal of information on magic and mysticism. According to his biographers, it was this document that inspired Cagliostro to delve yet deeper into the arcane mysteries of the occult.

Following yet another peripatetic trip through Holland, Italy and Germany, Cagliostro visited another legendary occult figure, the Comte de St Germain. In a bizarre episode, the Comte agreed to receive Cagliostro and Lorenza at two o'clock in the morning, at which time they arrived at his 'temple of mystery', dressed in white robes. The drawbridge was lowered, and they were greeted by an exceptionally tall man who led them to a dimly lit room, where folded doors sprang open to reveal a temple illuminated by hundreds of candles. The Comte de St Germain sat upon the altar. At his feet sat two acolytes who swung golden censers.

The Comte wore a diamond-studded pentagram upon his chest. On the steps leading to the altar stood a statue holding a vase bearing the inscription 'Elixir of Immortality'. An enormous mirror hung on one wall, above which were the words 'Store House of Wandering Souls'. The profound silence in the room was broken by the Comte, who asked the couple who they were, where they came from, and what they wanted. Cagliostro and Lorenza then prostrated themselves before the Comte, and Cagliostro declared, 'I come to invoke the God of the faithful, the Son of Nature, the Sire of Truth. I come to demand of him one of the fourteen thousand seven hundred secrets which are treasured in his breast, I come to proclaim myself his slave, his apostle, his martyr.'

After a long pause, the Comte asked what Lorenza wanted, to which she replied, 'To obey and to serve.'

A man dressed in a long mantle appeared, telling them that the ultimate goal of the Comte and his followers was the government of humanity. He then withdrew, and an extremely tall man led the two supplicants to the feet of the Comte, who proceeded to tell them how he had long ago grown disillusioned with all the affairs with which humanity concerned itself. Politics, science, theology, philosophy and history were all the ridiculous amusements of a dullard race. It was only through the discovery of magic that the Comte perceived the true vastness and majesty of the Universe.

The encounter ended with a sumptuous feast, during which the couple were entreated to avoid so-called men of learning, and to spread the teachings of the Comte among the rest of humanity.

Following his establishment of several Masonic Lodges (and his acceptance of the gifts and money that came with such establishments), Cagliostro travelled to St Petersburg, where he quickly made a reputation for himself as an effective physician. Spence notes that there has been a great deal of controversy concerning the large number of cures that were attributed to Cagliostro, adding that the likeliest explanation is 'a species of mesmeric influence', or hypnotism. 'It has been said that he trusted simply to the laying on of hands; that he charged nothing for his services; that most of his time was occupied in treating the poor, among whom he distributed vast amounts of money.'

When he returned to Germany, Cagliostro found himself greatly admired as a benefactor of humanity, although some suspected that his cures were the result of sorcery rather than miracles. Cagliostro himself invariably claimed that they were performed with the assistance of God.

Cagliostro remained at Strasburg for three years, during which time he cultivated a close friendship with the Cardinal-

Archbishop, Louis de Rohan. De Rohan belonged to one of the most important and illustrious families in France. Greedy, arrogant and debauched, he enjoyed a lifestyle that was scandalous by any standards, having many affairs. He was also an extremely gullible man who was obsessed with alchemy, and who thus was a prime target for Cagliostro. It is said that he succeeded in transmuting base metal to gold under the rapt gaze of de Rohan, who evidently was impressed enough to shower him with money. Nor had he any doubt that Cagliostro possessed the secret of eternal youth, the Elixir of Immortality, and built a house in which he intended to receive it.

When he had relieved de Rohan of the vast majority of his funds, Cagliostro decided it was once again time to be on his way; and so he set off first for Bordeaux, then to Lyons where he established a Masonic headquarters, and then to Paris. Here he became known as a 'master of practical magic', with the power to invoke phantoms, which appeared in vases of water or mirrors. Of course, trickery is to be suspected, although some historians of the occult, including A. E. Waite, believe that the visions were similar to those of crystal-gazing, and that Cagliostro himself was astonished at his success in the invocation of spirits. In any event, he became famous throughout Paris as the 'Divine Cagliostro', and was even introduced to the court of Louis XVI.

Cagliostro and Lorenza took full advantage of the air of mystery surrounding them. They lived in an isolated house surrounded by huge gardens. While Cagliostro conducted various magical and alchemical experiments in his laboratory, Lorenza maintained an intense privacy, and only appeared very occasionally before groups of carefully selected admirers. She hosted magical suppers to which the Parisian élite waited breathlessly to be invited, and at which seances would be conducted with the intention of communicating with the illustrious dead.

However, the evocation of the dead without doubt took second place to the spreading of Cagliostro's rite of Egyptian Masonry. His lodges admitted women as well as men, with the former being instructed by Lorenza, the Grand Mistress of the Order. Cagliostro himself took the title of Grand Copt. It hardly need be said that membership of the Order came at a price, and Cagliostro's coffers swelled enormously, courtesy of the powerful and wealthy who flocked to join. A confidence trickster of great skill he may have been, but, as Spence noted above, Cagliostro did not keep his vast wealth entirely to himself: he also gave away huge sums to the poor and needy, and did his best to ensure that the sick were taken care of.

Naturally, much mystery surrounds the Masonic rites that were practised at the headquarters in the Faubourg Saint Honoré. In his *Encyclopaedia of Occultism*, Lewis Spence offers some information on the nature of the female initiations. The initiates were required to take off their clothes and put on white robes. They were then taken into a temple containing thirty-six armchairs covered with black satin. Here they found Lorenza, clothed in white, seated upon a throne, on either side of which stood a tall figure dressed in such a manner that their sex could not be determined. As the light was gradually lowered, Lorenza commanded the initiates to uncover their left legs up to the thigh, and to raise their right arms and rest them on neighbouring pillars. Two young women then entered carrying swords, and bound the initiates together with silk ropes.

After a lengthy silence, Lorenza gave an impassioned speech on the necessity of the emancipation of women from the bonds that had been imposed upon them throughout history, and which were symbolised by the silk ropes binding the initiates. When the speech was over, the women were freed from their bindings, and were led to separate rooms, and then out into the garden. Some were pursued by men who harangued them with unthinkably lewd solicitations, while others experienced the altogether more pleasant attentions of men who threw themselves sighing at their feet.

When these rites were over, the initiates returned to the temple and were congratulated by Lorenza. At this point, a skylight in the roof opened and Cagliostro descended into the room, perched upon a golden sphere with a serpent in his hand and a star upon his head. Lorenza introduced him to the initiates as the genius of Truth, the divine Cagliostro, the repository of all knowledge. He then commanded the women to disrobe, for if they were to receive truth, they should be as naked as truth itself. Lorenza also let her robes fall to the ground, and watched as Cagliostro proceeded to dispense his wisdom. The magical arts, he said, were the secret of humanity's salvation and ultimate happiness. Such was the completeness of this happiness that it was not confined solely to the spiritual, but to the material also.

When he had finished his speech, Cagliostro seated himself once more upon the golden sphere, and disappeared through the ceiling. The completion of the proceedings was marked with a ball – a rather bizarre conclusion, but perhaps one that was in keeping with the extravagant theatrics of the rite itself.

It is perhaps fitting (and certainly unsurprising) that a man such as Cagliostro should have become implicated in one of history's most preposterous and famous scandals.

It began when the royal jewellers, Boehmer and Bassenge, created what was quite probably the most elaborate and valuable piece of jewellery in the world, a golden necklace containing no fewer than 647 diamonds. It had been intended for the notoriously ostentatious Madame du Barry, the mistress of King Louis XV of France. In today's currency, the necklace would have cost between five and ten million pounds.

Unfortunately for Boehmer and Bassenge, Louis XV died of smallpox before payment for the necklace was made. The jewellers had tied up their entire assets in the production of the necklace, and feared that if another buyer could not be found, they would be ruined. Fortunately, Marie Antoinette, the wife of Louis XVI, was fully the equal of Madame du Barry when it came to extravagance, and so Boehmer tried desperately to sell her the necklace. Astonishingly, however, she declined.

Boehmer was crestfallen, and wept in front of the queen, saying that his career was at an end, and even threatening to take his own life. Marie Antoinette responded with sound good sense that the solution was simple enough: the necklace should be broken up and the diamonds sold separately. Boehmer could not bring himself to destroy his exquisite work, however, and approached the royal court of Spain in search of a buyer, without luck.

Perhaps the most important character in the whole affair was the seductive and unscrupulous adventuress Jeanne de Valois. Having heard of Cardinal de Rohan's disgracefully hedonistic lifestyle, Jeanne managed to get herself invited to one of his castles, and it was not long before he fell prey to her charms. Jeanne's husband, a dashing gendarme named Nicolas de Lamotte, was heavily in debt; she had de Rohan pay off his bad debts and promote him to captain in the dragoons. In one of her most daring scams, she went to Versailles and pretended to faint in a reception room. Nicolas explained to the concerned courtiers that she was of royal blood, and was suffering from malnutrition. This incredible audacity was rewarded with a large annual pension.

For Jeanne, who by now had started calling herself the Comtesse de Lamotte-Valois, the success of each escapade spurred her on to acts of even greater trickery and mischief. It was at this time that she met Cagliostro, who told her of Cardinal de Rohan's desire to gain acceptance at the court of Versailles, and despair of ever doing so owing to the queen's intense dislike of him.

It is unclear how Cagliostro and Jeanne met, or even why he told her of Rohan's desire for royal recognition, a weakness she would certainly be able to exploit. Perhaps he simply recognised a kindred spirit, and happily supplied her with this information about the contemptible cardinal.

Never one to miss an opportunity, Jeanne began to drop hints to the cardinal that she and the queen were great friends, promising him that at the next court event Marie Antoinette would nod to him. During the event, de Rohan watched for the queen's gesture; so anxious was he to see it that he imagined he did, and rewarded Jeanne with money for helping to bring about this change in the queen's attitude. With the help of her husband's friend Retaux de Villette, who acted as her secretary (and who was also her lover), Jeanne forged notes on gilded paper with the royal fleur-de-lis, which helped to convince de Rohan that the queen had changed her mind about him.

De Rohan was falling further and further under Jeanne's spell, and, in possession of Cagliostro's information, she searched for a scheme that would ensnare him completely. Eventually she came up with her most audacious and potentially dangerous scam to date. With the help of de Lamotte, she arranged a secret meeting between de Rohan and the 'queen' near the Grove of Venus in Marie Antoinette's private gardens, which were out of bounds to anyone who did not have her permission to be there, including the king.

Lamotte paid a visit to one of the favourite haunts of Parisian prostitutes and introduced himself to a young woman named Nicole who bore a resemblance to the queen, and who was not blessed with much in the way of intelligence. They dressed the girl in a white gown, which exactly resembled one worn by Marie Antoinette in one of her most well-known portraits, and coached her on what to say when she met de Rohan. There was, of course, no conceivable way that the girl could carry off a convincing impersonation of Marie Antoinette; but according to Jeanne's plan, she would not need to. The most fleeting contact was all that was needed.

Jeanne was careful to choose an evening on which there was no moon for the secret rendezvous. His heart full of hope for his future at the royal court, the greedy and gullible de Rohan entered the queen's private gardens, moving in silent expectation like a thief or a spy among the trees. When he saw the 'queen', he emerged from his cover, approached her and bowed deeply.

Struggling to remember the single line she had been given to say, the dim-witted Nicole whispered, 'You may hope that the past will be forgotten.' This was as long a speech as Jeanne dared risk, and with that the plan moved swiftly into its next phase. Before de Rohan could breathe another word, a manservant in palace livery rushed up to the couple and begged the 'queen' to return to the palace immediately. As he did so, he made certain that de Rohan saw his face, even in the darkness of the moonless night.

Now Jeanne well and truly had a long-term, profitable dupe. Just as Cagliostro had done, she and de Lamotte proceeded to tap de Rohan for money at every opportunity. On one occasion, for instance, she reported to the Cardinal that the queen was anxious to help out an impoverished noble family, but could not do so due to her own shortage of funds. De Rohan immediately obliged with a gift of 50,000 livres, although he was himself deeply in debt, and had to pawn his household goods to keep up with Jeanne's subtle requests for money.

It was at this point that Boehmer and Bassenge decided to try once more to sell their ridiculously extravagant diamond necklace to the queen. Rumours regarding the Valois' close friendship with Marie Antoinette had continued to spread, and so the jewellers approached the couple, asking them if they might try to persuade her that the necklace was something she absolutely could not do without.

To Jeanne, this had the potential to be her most lucrative scam so far, and so she immediately contacted de Rohan, telling him that the queen wished him to provide security for the purchase of the necklace. When she added that the queen had agreed to pay 1,600,000 livres in four half-yearly instalments, the Cardinal's blood drained from his face; nevertheless, he added his signature to the agreement. The necklace was duly delivered to de Rohan's house, and shortly afterwards a manservant presented himself, informing the Cardinal that, by order of the queen, he was to take the necklace to the palace. This was the same man who had bid the 'queen' return to the palace on the evening de Rohan had met her in her private gardens, and who had made certain that the Cardinal clearly saw his face.

With the necklace now in her possession, Jeanne lost no time in doing what Marie Antoinette herself had advised Boehmer to do when she had declined to purchase it. She broke it up, prying the diamonds from their settings with an old penknife and selling them separately.

When the date of the first instalment of 400,000 livres became due, Boehmer went to see de Rohan, who of course was utterly unable to pay. Noting the Cardinal's anxiety, and sharing his belief that Marie Antoinette possessed the necklace, Boehmer went to Versailles, where he met one of the queen's ladies-in-waiting. When he mentioned the diamond necklace, the lady asked him what he was talking about: the queen had certainly not purchased any such necklace.

Knowing now that something was terribly wrong, Boehmer went to see Jeanne, who laughed in his face and told him that the affair had nothing whatsoever to do with her. He would be best advised, she said, to go back to the Cardinal and get the money from him. His head filled with awful visions of financial ruin, Boehmer went instead directly to King Louis XVI. The king listened to the jeweller's story in amazement. Marie Antoinette was also present, and when he turned to ask her if she knew anything of this affair, she shouted indignantly that Boehmer had been pestering her to buy the necklace, but she had refused. What angered her more than anything, however, was that the detested de Rohan should be connected with the scandal. She demanded that he be arrested, along with all the other culprits, including Cagliostro and Lorenza, whom Jeanne accused of stealing the necklace.

Jeanne made all manner of claims against Cagliostro, including that he was a confidence trickster and a false prophet. It did not take him long, however, to prove his entire innocence of the charges of theft made against him, and at his trial he provided the galvanised public with what Lewis Spence calls 'one of the most romantic and fanciful, if manifestly absurd, life stories in the history of autobiography'. His outrageously bloated and embellished account of his life, delivered in court, illustrated his delightfully fertile and self-aggrandising imagination.

Everyone in the court thought his life story hilarious, including the judges. Although he was acquitted of any wrongdoing, his very innocence made him yet more enemies in high places. Nevertheless, he was a hero to the people, who remembered the kindness and generosity with which he had treated them.

Jeanne de Valois did not fare so well. Both Retaux de Villette and the prostitute Nicole told everything they knew about her (Nicolas de Lamotte had already fled the country and was never seen again). The punishment suffered by Jeanne further damaged the already tarnished reputation of Marie Antoinette. Jeanne was sentenced to be flogged, branded with a 'V' for *voleuse* (thief) and then imprisoned for life. When the time came for her to be branded, Jeanne struggled so fiercely that it took thirteen men to hold her down. Even then she did not cease. In the violence of the struggle, her clothes were ripped and the branding iron accidentally scorched her breast.

News of these dreadful events quickly spread, arousing near-universal sympathy for the comtesse. Huge numbers of people went to the Bastille to visit her, including the highest of Parisian society. A few weeks later, Jeanne managed to escape from prison disguised as a boy, and fled to England, where she took her own life by jumping from the window of a brothel in 1791. Cardinal de Rohan was acquitted, but was banished from court and forced to spend the rest of his life in anonymity in the country-side far from Versailles.

Cagliostro and Lorenza were released, and shortly afterwards went to London, where he wrote an open letter to the French people. The letter, which was circulated widely, predicted the French Revolution, the destruction of the Bastille and the down-fall of the monarchy – events that were perhaps hastened by the affair of the diamond necklace.

Not long after Cagliostro's arrival in London, an exposé of his life was printed in *Courier de l'Europe*, a French newspaper published there. His reputation was irreparably damaged, prompting further wanderings through Switzerland, Austria and finally Italy. In Rome he found himself welcomed at first. He continued his studies in medicine and lived quietly with Lorenza. However, once again he made a mistake, which cost him the goodwill of his hosts. His intention was to establish a Masonic lodge in the Eternal City itself, which of course inspired the wrath of the Roman Catholic Church. On 27 September 1789 Cagliostro was arrested by order of the Holy Inquisition and imprisoned in the Castle of Saint Angelo.

Following an interrogation that lasted fully eighteen months, he was sentenced to death on 7 April 1791. This sentence was commuted to life imprisonment by order of the Pope, and the sentence to be served in the castle in which he had been interrogated. He made a desperate attempt to escape on one occasion. Requesting the presence of a confessor, he attacked the priest sent to him, intending to strangle him and take his habit as a disguise in which to flee the castle. The priest, however, was too strong, and it was Cagliostro who was overpowered.

Cagliostro was transferred to the remote Castle of San Leo near Montefeltro, where he died and was buried in 1795. The exact cause of his death is unknown; however, the conditions in which he was kept can have done little to prolong his life. The castle's galleries, which had been cut from solid rock, were divided into cells. In 1791, Cagliostro was imprisoned in one of the old dried-up cisterns that had been converted to serve as dungeons for the worst criminals. Although the sentence of death that the Inquisition had passed on him had been commuted to life imprisonment by the Holy Tribunal, it was stipulated that the commutation should be equivalent to a death sentence. Cagliostro was kept in complete isolation; his only sight of another human being was when the jailers opened the trap door in the ceiling of his dungeon and dropped food down to him. For three years he languished in this dreadful hole, until the prison governor took pity on him and had him moved to a cell on ground level. His time in the dungeon had proved too much for him, however, and he died a few months later.

Lorenza suffered a similar fate. Sentenced by the Inquisition to imprisonment for life, she was incarcerated in the Convent of Saint Appolonia, a women's prison in Rome, where she apparently died in 1794.

Although most historians agree that Cagliostro was Giuseppe Balsamo, others, such as W. R. H. Trowbridge, maintain that this is not the case, and that the identification of Cagliostro with Balsamo is the result of the exposé by the editor of *Courier de l'Europe*, 'a person of the lowest and most profligate habits', according to Lewis Spence. Whatever his true identity, whether he possessed genuine magical ability or whether his true talent lay simply in separating the gullible from their money, the great eighteenth-century rake known as Cagliostro was without doubt one of the most charismatic figures in European occultism.

SEVEN

The Ritualist

'I was awakened to the knowledge that I possessed a magical means of becoming conscious of and satisfying a part of my nature, which had up to that moment concealed itself from me. It was an experience of horror and pain, combined with a certain ghostly terror, yet at the same time it was the key to the purest and holiest spiritual ecstasy that exists.'

ALEISTER CROWLEY, *THE BOOK OF THE LAW*

All magic works on the belief that sound (be it expressed in words or names) has genuine power to effect change in accordance with the magician's will. The name of a god, angel or demon contains within it magical energy, a divine power that can be directed and utilised in rituals. There is also a belief that there is a secret name – an ultimate word of power – that when properly used will convey power over everything in the Universe.

Among the most potent of the Names of Power is the personal name of God, which is so sacred that it is very rarely pronounced aloud. It is known as the Tetragrammaton, which means 'word of four letters'. The four Hebrew letters translate to: yod, he, vau, he, or YHVH. The correct pronunciation of this word is uncertain, mainly because it was spoken so rarely that no pronunciation tradition survives. Since correct pronunciation is absolutely essential in magical operations, only a very few magicians have been able to discover the secret and to use it properly.

Although the Tetragrammaton contains great power, there is an even more powerful word, the Shemhamforash. This was the name, containing seventy-two syllables, that Moses used to part the Red Sea when the Israelites were fleeing Egypt. No one knows how to pronounce this fearsome word of power.

Some devotees of the cabbala, the immensely complex system of Hebrew mysticism, have connected the Shemhamforash with the Tetragrammaton using gematria, or the assigning of numerical values to letters. According to gematria, the numerical equivalents of YHVH are 10, 5, 6, 5, which when added together equal 26. However, by building up the Tetragrammaton in progressive stages, the total is found to be 72, the number of syllables in the Shemhamforash:

$$
\begin{array}{ll}
Y & = 10 \\
YH & = 15 \\
YHV & = 21 \\
YHVH & = 26 \\
\hline
& 72
\end{array}
$$

It is not enough to know the Names of Power: the magician must also know how and when to use them. According to the magician Israel Regardie, at the appropriate time in the ritual, one should inhale deeply, drawing the air steadily into the lungs, while imagining that one is simultaneously drawing in the name itself. The name should be envisaged as hanging in the air in front of the magician, written in fire, and be drawn down through the body, through the lungs, stomach, legs and feet, thus filling the entire body with the fire of the name.

In speaking (or rather shouting) the name, the magician should draw it back up from his feet, through his legs, stomach and lungs, then cry it out triumphantly. If he has done this correctly, the magician should feel his body full of a powerful psychic energy in which the name is magically vibrated. This vibration extends into the astral light, the divine substance that permeates the Universe. The spirit invoked should respond to this vibration, and declare its presence to the magician.

While orthodox science would have serious problems accepting that the practice of magic yields measurable results, it does accept that sound waves do affect the environment. In their book *Mysteries of Magic*, Stuart Holroyd and Neil Powell cite experiments conducted by a Swiss physicist, Hans Jenny, which he described in an article entitled 'Visualising Sound' in a 1968 issue of *Science Journal*:

> Jenny coined the term 'cymatics' for the study of the effects of sound waves on matter. His work was a development of that of the eighteenth-century physicist Ernst Chladni, who discovered that sand scattered on a metal plate will arrange itself in beautiful patterns at certain sounds from a violin. Jenny extended his research to the human voice. He invented a machine that he called the 'tonoscope', which converts sound to three-dimensional forms. He discovered that the sound of the letter O produces a perfect sphere – exactly the shape that we use for the sound in our script. Jenny's research has shown that sounds – and therefore also words and names – have properties and powers of their own. This is something that occultists and magicians have never doubted.

Holroyd and Powell go on to note that the magical belief in the constructive power of sound is illustrated in the Book of Genesis: 'The Universe was created by the *Word* of God.' It needed the expression of the Word to give reality to the divine intention. The use of magical Names and Words of Power is thus the means by which human beings can tap into the hidden energy sources of the Universe.

This belief is also a key element in Buddhism and Hinduism. The mantras are word and sound constructions, which give the speaker control over the worlds of the spirit. These words and verses were either composed, or came via lengthy meditation.

The mantras often rely on compression to gain their power. For example, a holy book might be condensed into a single chapter. This summary would then be further reduced to a few sentences, then a single line, and finally to one word or even a single syllable. The essence of an entire book would thus be contained within one sound.

Mantras are used with the understanding that the entire Universe is based on sound vibrations, and that their judicious use can bring great power, both to heal and to destroy. Mantras can be used as magical spells, and fantastic powers are said to accompany the repetition of some of them, such as the binding of other people to one's will, and even the ability to travel anywhere in the Universe. Many mantras are based on sounds that end with an M or an N, the most famous of which is, of course, *Om*, which represents all the sounds of the Universe.

The use of Words of Power represents what is known as 'high' or 'ritual magic', in which the practitioner uses his knowledge in an attempt to commune with the divine powers of the Universe. Its counterpart is known as 'low magic', an altogether more tawdry and dangerous pursuit, in which the practitioner uses magical spells and incantations solely for personal gain, be it in love, war, or the base accumulation of material wealth.

The spells used in both high and low magic often require the use of various ingredients, the most important of which are plants and herbs. Mandrake is the most well known of the plants thought to possess magical properties. Although this plant is found throughout the world, the true mandrake, *mandragora*, grows only around the Mediterranean. With its curiously human-shaped root, the mandrake has been sought for its putative aphrodisiac properties, as well as its ability to heal many ailments.

According to accepted wisdom, the most powerful specimens grew beneath gallows, nourished by the semen, which is frequently ejaculated when a man is hanged. They were considered to be more akin to animals than plants, and to take them from the ground was potentially very dangerous, for they would utter a piercing shriek that would strike any listener dead. For this reason, dogs were often used to unearth them. One end of the rope would be attached to the mandrake, and the other to the dog's neck. Pieces of food would then be thrown just out of the dog's reach, and in attempting to reach it the animal would pull the root out of the earth. The cry of the mandrake would kill the dog instantly, while those who sought the mandrake would look on with ears well blocked. They would then take the mandrake from the ground and bury the dog in its place.

The belief that semen offers particularly good nourishment to the plant resulted in its being prized as an effective ingredient in love potions. One of the more charming love spells is known as Lover's Mandrake. When he has found the mandrake, the lover must dig it up before dawn during the waxing of the moon. (Fortunately for the lover, this spell is not based on the legend that the root utters a lethal scream when plucked from the soil.) He utters the words, 'Blessed be this earth, this root, this night.' He then takes the root home and trims it until it is as close to the female form as he can make it. Holding it in his left hand, he makes the sign of the pentagram with his right and gives the mandrake the name of the one he loves.

Next, he buries the root in his garden and pours over it a mixture of water, milk and some of his own blood, while intoning, 'Blood and milk upon the grave / Will make —— evermore my slave.' He leaves the root in the ground until the next new Moon, and then digs it up one hour before sunrise, saying, 'Moon above so palely shining / Bestow this night thy sacred blessing / On my prayer and ritual plea / To fill ——'s heart with love for me.'

For the next several weeks, the lover must allow the mandrake to dry out completely, during which time he must frequently pass it through a special type of incense associated with the goddess Venus while chanting, 'This fruit is scorched by that same heat / Which warms my heart with every beat.'

At the end of the drying-out process, the lover focuses his concentration upon the loved one, and thrusts a silver pin through the mandrake-figure's heart. The operation complete, he leaves the figure on a window sill so that it will be bathed in the light of the moon.

The most straightforward spells are those described in the grimoires, the medieval books of black magic, one of which requires the lover to look deeply into the woman's eyes, and chant, 'Kaphe, kasita, non Kapheta et publica filii omnibus suis.' The spell includes a postscript: 'Do not be surprised at or ashamed of these enigmatical words whose occult meaning you do not know; for if you pronounce them with sufficient faith you will very soon possess her love.' While such a ludicrous chant may or may not have impressed a woman in medieval times, it would have a modern woman (quite rightly) heading quickly for the nearest door.

The medieval grimoires also contain spells to satisfy the base desires of the lecher. The *Grimorium Verum*, for instance, contains a spell to compel a woman to dance naked against her will. The operation is simple enough: the man writes the word *Frutimiere* in bat's blood on a piece of virgin parchment, which is then laid on a stone over which a Mass has been said, and placed at the back of a door. If the woman walks past that door, she will be compelled to walk through the door, take off her clothes and dance wildly.

There are all manner of such spells in the books of black magic. One of the more gruesome requires the magician to take a dove's heart, a sparrow's liver, a swallow's womb and a hare's kidney, dry them and grind them to a fine powder. He must then add an equal quantity of his own blood, leave the mixture to dry, and then make the woman he desires eat it. She will then be totally submissive to him ... although she would surely have to be very submissive to eat such a filthy concoction in the first place!

To ensure a woman does not desire one's rival in love, one must take the genitals of a wolf and combine them with hairs taken from the rival's cheeks, eyebrows and beard, burn them, reduce them to powder, and then mix them with water and give the potion to the woman to drink. This potion sounds as disgusting as that in the previous example, and it seems more likely to drive the woman into the rival's arms than bind her to the magician.

To force a woman to speak truthfully, the magician must enter her bedroom while she is asleep, armed with the tongue of a live toad, which he has just torn out, and place it on her heart. Talking in her sleep, she will then answer any question he puts to her – assuming she does not wake up and immediately call the police.

Many written spells utilise palindromes, which magicians believe to contain great magical power. When they are arranged in a square, the power of these palindromes is greatly increased. Among the most powerful of these magic squares is the Sator formula, in which the words remain the same whichever way they are read:

```
S A T O R
A R E P O
T E N E T
O P E R A
R O T A S
```

This formula was discovered on fragments of plaster from the wall of a Roman villa in Cirencester, and has also been found in ancient Bibles and drinking vessels. It has many uses, including detecting witches (for no witch can remain in a room with it), for protecting milk against witchcraft, and even for extinguishing fires (the formula should be written on a wooden plate and thrown into the flames).

No one knows exactly what the words of the Sator formula mean, although many attempts have been made to explain them. One, for instance, explains it as follows: 'Arepo, the sower (sator), delays (tenet) the wheels (rotas) by his works (opera).' Another: 'The sower is at the plough (arepo), the work occupies the wheels.' Mathers claimed that it could be translated thus: 'The Creator (sator), slow-moving (arepo) maintains (tenet) His creations (opera) as vortices (rotas).'

There are many spells that do not rely upon words or written symbols for their efficacy, but instead upon the system of correspondences upon which the entire magical system rests. Herbs, of course, are among the most important ingredients in the inventory of magical accoutrements, and sage is a particularly useful herb. Sage is associated with Jupiter and Venus, and can be used to produce a versatile powder. It should be picked during the Sun's passage through Leo, and then ground into a powder and buried in a pot in a heap of dung for thirty days. Upon retrieving it, the magician will discover that it has turned into a quantity of worms, which he should then burn between two red-hot bricks and grind into powder. The substance is then ready for use. If sprinkled on the magician's feet, it will compel any powerful person to grant his request. Placed under the magician's tongue, it will cause anyone he kisses to fall helplessly in love with him. Anyone sitting in the light of a lamp whose oil contains the powder will suffer the illusion of the room being filled with serpents.

The *Grimorium Verum* contains a magical formula for doubling one's money, although the very first step might prove too daunting for many. One must pluck a hair from near the vulva of a mare in heat, chanting, 'Drigne, Dragne, Dragne.' The hair must be placed in an earthenware pot with a lid, which has been filled with water from a spring, and then hidden away for nine days. When he opens the pot when this period has expired, the magician will find, instead of the hair, a tiny snake writhing in the pot. When the snake rears up at the magician, he must say, 'I accept the pact.' He must then place the little snake in a box made of new pine and feed it every day with wheat husks. The box is now ready, and whenever the magician wants money, he must put some coins in with the snake, and then go and lie down for three hours or so. When he gets up and looks in the box, he will find that the money has doubled. Although the grimoire cautions against attempting to gain more than 100 coins in this manner, it adds that occasionally the snake will have a human face, and if this happens, up to 1,000 coins may be obtained.

The successful wizard is therefore well aware of the importance of sound when fashioned into the Words of Power that drive magical operations. And no magician understood this importance more profoundly than Aleister Crowley. Few figures in the world of the occult have provoked as much controversy as this man, the self-styled 'Great Beast' who was called the 'wickedest man in the world' by the British press (a description in which he revelled). An in-depth analysis of his life, work and thought would require a book in itself, perhaps several, and for this reason we must content ourselves with an all-too-brief overview of one who is among the most sinister and charismatic of magicians.

Aleister Crowley was born on 12 October 1875 at Leamington Spa, Warwickshire into a wealthy, religious family. (He had a baby sister who died in infancy.) The year of his birth, the great French occultist Eliphas Levi died, and Crowley later became convinced that he was a reincarnation of Levi. (He also believed that he had been Cagliostro in a previous life.) His father, Edward, a successful brewer, was a preacher in the Plymouth Brethren, and Crowley received a strict Christian upbringing against which he rebelled at every opportunity. In 1881 the family moved to Redhill in Surrey, and three years later Crowley was sent to an evangelist school at St Leonards, and then to a school in Cambridge the following year. His father died in 1887, and Crowley was removed from the school two years later. During those two years he was severely mistreated to the extent that his health was undermined, and this is certainly one of the factors in his lifelong hatred of and contempt for Christianity.

Crowley was educated at Malvern, Tonbridge and Trinity College, Cambridge. Initially he intended to become a chemist, and also entertained the notion of entering the diplomatic service. However, he became interested in religious studies, and with his discovery of alchemy the course of his life changed irrevocably. While he was at Cambridge, the trust fund that had been set up on the death of his father matured, offering Crowley financial freedom and independence from his family. He immediately left university.

Crowley was a keen (and excellent) mountaineer, and during a climbing trip to the Alps he met another Englishman in a bar. On hearing of Crowley's intense interest in alchemy, the man offered to introduce him to another of similar interests. Back in England, Crowley was introduced to the Hermetic Order of the Golden Dawn, which he joined in 1898, taking as his magical name Brother Perdurabo (I shall endure). The Golden Dawn was led by Samuel Liddell Mathers, and its membership included several luminaries of the time, including W. B. Yeats, Arthur Machen, Algernon Blackwood, A. E. Waite, Sax Rohmer and Bram Stoker. Membership also included the Astronomer Royal of Scotland, and an elderly clergyman who had succeeded in making the Elixir of Life thirty years earlier, but had been too frightened to drink it.

The Golden Dawn is perhaps the most famous of all magical societies; to call it legendary would be an understatement. There is some debate as to the precise origins of the order, but the version that seems to enjoy the widest agreement is that it was created by William Wynn Westcott, a London coroner and Freemason, who was head of the esoteric Societas Rosicruciana in Anglia. Dissatisfied with the society's lack of interest in performing practical ritual magic, Westcott left to found his own magical order. He was faced with an immediate problem, however: by their very nature, occult orders required some form of provenance, an origin in the distant past, a supernatural pedigree. Fortunately, the solution to this problem lay in a mysterious manuscript allegedly discovered in 1887 by a colleague, Dr Woodman, in a bookshop. The manuscript was written in cipher. Samuel Mathers managed to translate it with the help of his clairvoyant wife Moina, and discovered that it was a treatise on the Tarot and other mystical matters. It also contained the address of a Fräulein Anna Sprengel in Nuremberg, Germany.

Westcott contacted Anna Sprengel, who responded by sending him a charter for a new lodge of her order of Rosicrucian adepts: the Isis-Urania Lodge of the Hermetic Order of the Golden Dawn, which opened on 20 March 1888. The Golden

Dawn was divided into eleven degrees or grades, representing stages of increased occult learning and ability. The degrees were based upon the Cabbalistic Tree of Life, and were further divided into three classes: the first, called the Golden Dawn, included those who had basic magical knowledge; the second, called the Red Rose and Golden Cross, included those who were able to put their knowledge to practical magical use; and the third was known as the Silver Star, and included those of considerable ability, who had travelled into the astral realms and returned with their sanity intact.

The nature of the work undertaken in the lower grades was primarily academic, with members learning about the principles of yoga, the astral plane, the tarot, Enochian magic and so on. In the middle grades, emphasis was placed on making contact with one's Holy Guardian Angel. This was of extreme importance, since it allowed the magician to reach his full potential and become a Master.

Around 1891, Anna Sprengel died, and representatives of the German order wrote to the Golden Dawn in London, informing them that they had all that they needed to carry their work forward. There was no further contact from them. Westcott took this to mean that they should endeavour to make contact with the Secret Chiefs, a mysterious group of immensely powerful adepts who were said to be immortal and lived somewhere in Tibet.

In 1891, Mathers claimed to have made contact with the Secret Chiefs in the Bois de Boulogne, Paris, and further announced that they had granted him sole authority to rule the order. He promptly took control from Westcott, who resigned in 1897. With the other leader of the Golden Dawn, Dr Woodman, already dead, there was no one to stand in Mathers's way.

Mathers was then living in Paris with Moina, whose brother was the philosopher Henri Bergson (whom Mathers had tried unsuccessfully to convert to magic). Their house was elaborately decorated in the manner of an Egyptian temple, and here they celebrated 'Egyptian Masses', invoking the goddess Isis. According to the occult historian Richard Cavendish:

Mathers officiated in a long white robe, a metal belt engraved with the signs of the zodiac, bracelets round his wrists and ankles, and a leopard-skin slung across his shoulders. He was convinced that he was descended from the Scottish clan MacGregor and took to calling himself MacGregor Mathers, Chevalier MacGregor and Comte de Glenstrae. W. B. Yeats, whose magical name in the Golden Dawn was Daemon est Deus Inversus (The Devil is God Reversed), was a frequent visitor to the Mathers household in Paris. In the evenings they used to play a peculiar form of chess for four players. Yeats and Mrs Mathers played against Mathers and a spirit. Before moving his spirit-partner's piece Mathers would shade his eyes and stare earnestly at the spirit's empty chair at the other side of the board.

Mathers edited and translated several important magical books, including the *Key of Solomon*, the *Sacred Magic of Abramelin the Mage* and the *Kabbalah Unveiled*.

Crowley, the new recruit, moved in with another Golden Dawn member, an engineer named Allan Bennett. A formidable magician, Bennett carried a glass candlestick with him and once used it as a magical weapon against a Theosophist who cast doubt upon his powers. Apparently, it took fourteen hours for the paralysis of both mind and body to wear off. Bennett became Crowley's mentor and educated him in the practices of ritual magic. Under Bennett's guidance, Crowley began his first magical experiments in an apartment in Chancery Lane in London. Also present at these rituals was George Cecil Jones, another of Crowley's mentors, with whom he would later co-found his own magical society, the Argenteum Astrum, or the Order of the Silver Star (usually abbreviated as A.˙.A.˙.). Bennett later moved to Ceylon (present-day Sri Lanka) and became a Buddhist monk. In later years Crowley visited Bennett, and received training in Buddhism, yoga and meditation. Bennett died in 1923 during a missionary trip to bring Buddhism to the West.

Crowley was growing more and more irritated at the Golden

Dawn, whose members, he felt, were not taking their magic seriously enough. He was anxious to put his accumulated knowledge of the occult to some important use, and in 1899 bought Boleskine House on the shores of Loch Ness for the purpose of performing a powerful ritual known as the Abramelin Working. Dating from the fourteenth century, the purpose of this operation was to contact one's Holy Guardian Angel. So powerful and dangerous was the Abramelin Working that no one had attempted it for centuries. It was also extremely complicated, requiring six months of extreme concentration to perform.

Crowley might have managed to complete it, had he not met Rose Kelly halfway through. They were married immediately, and the Abramelin Working was abandoned.

During their honeymoon in Egypt in 1904, Crowley performed various occult rituals, one of which he conducted within the King's Chamber of the Great Pyramid. Apparently in consequence, Rose began to chant, repeating the phrase, 'They are waiting for you'. His new wife claimed that he had offended the Egyptian god Horus with his abandonment of the Abramelin Working.

Somewhat bemused by his new wife's sudden clairvoyant ability, Crowley began to ask various questions on arcane subjects, of which Rose could have had no possible prior knowledge. Her answers impressed him enough to take her to a museum where, after passing several statues of Horus without comment, Rose pointed to the Stele of Revealing, which contained an image of Horus. Of yet more interest to Crowley was the stele's catalogue number: 666, the number of the beast in the Book of Revelation. Crowley had used this number to refer to himself, calling himself To Mega Therion, the Great Beast.

For the next three days, Crowley wrote down the information Rose gave in her semi-trance state, and the result was the *Liber AL vel Legis*, *The Book of the Law*. The source of this book was a transhuman entity calling itself Aiwass. At last, Crowley believed, he had succeeded in contacting his Holy Guardian Angel. *The Book of the Law* became the principal document in Crowley's magical philosophy, and signalled the beginning of a 'New Aeon', the transition between the Age of Osiris and the Age of Horus, in which all the old religions of humanity were to become obsolete. At the core of this philosophy is the famous and much-quoted maxim 'Do what thou wilt shall be the whole of the Law'. This must rank as one of the most misunderstood statements in history. Crowley's critics always assumed that it meant 'you can do whatever you want, without regard for anyone else's well-being'. In fact, it meant nothing of the kind. Its true meaning could be described as an expression of a kind of occultist existentialism, an exhortation to humanity to take responsibility for its own actions; to empower itself by choosing its own course without wasting time and energy seeking instruction and approval from orthodox religions.

While still in Egypt, Rose discovered that she was pregnant. She later gave birth to a daughter, Lola Zaza. On a trip to Vietnam, Crowley abandoned them both, and Lola died of typhoid. Already an alcoholic, Rose was consumed with grief, and began a mental decline that ended in insanity.

Crowley's attitude to sex caused at least as much controversy as his magical activities (the two would later become integrated in his system of occult practice). To call him sexually liberated would be something of an understatement: he lost his virginity at fourteen with a family maid, and had contracted gonorrhoea from a prostitute by the age of seventeen. He soon discovered that he was bisexual, and had a strong liking for sadomasochism. As an undergraduate, he met a female impersonator named Jerome Pollitt, with whom he had a number of dalliances. Although considered obscene and highly dangerous in Crowley's day (in which homosexuality was of course illegal), his attitude, to the well-balanced modern mind, seems altogether healthier. Basically, he believed that one may please oneself, as long as one is not hurting others; and in fact, such liberty destroys sexual obsession rather than fomenting it.

Crowley and Mathers eventually became bitter enemies, partly because of a letter Crowley wrote announcing the arrival of the Equinox of the Gods, and his own new status as the supreme magical authority. In addition, dissent had arisen from those members of the Golden Dawn who demanded proof of Mathers's agreement with the Secret Chiefs that it should be he who ran the order. The two men waged a magical war with each other, the prize being control of the Golden Dawn. When he realised what Crowley was up to, a furious Mathers apparently summoned a vampire and set it to attack him; but Crowley turned the creature's evil against it and defeated it. Mathers then used magic to strike dead Crowley's pack of bloodhounds, and then took away the sanity of his rival's servant, so that she attacked and attempted to kill Rose. The crazed servant finally had to be subdued with a salmon gaff. Crowley responded by summoning the demon Beelzebub and forty-nine attendant devils, and sent them to Paris to have words with Mathers. (Indeed, when Mathers died in 1918, many of his friends placed the blame firmly with Crowley, whom they suspected of using black magic to do away with him.)

Crowley was finally expelled from the Golden Dawn, partly through the efforts of W. B. Yeats, who strongly disapproved of his magical methods. In 1907, Crowley founded the A.˙.A.˙.. By 1914, however, he had only managed to recruit thirty-eight members. When Mathers obtained a court order preventing Crowley from publishing the Golden Dawn's secrets in his occult periodical *The Equinox*, Crowley appealed against it, using a talisman for 'gaining the affection of a judge'. To add insult to injury, Crowley took the talisman from the *Sacred Magic of Abramelin the Mage*, which Mathers had translated. The talisman worked, and Crowley's appeal was successful.

According to Richard Cavendish, modern magicians find the incantations of the magical grimoires 'crude and tedious'. Crowley himself claimed to have invoked spirits with the use of these rituals, but it was uncertain just how helpful they actually were. As a result, Crowley developed his own rituals, including the *Liber Samekh*. It is worth pausing here to describe this ritual, since it illustrates the principal concern of the magician: to invoke the divine power within himself in the guise of a disembodied 'spirit'. Basing his ritual on a Graeco-Egyptian magical text, Crowley used it in a series of magical workings in 1911 and 1921.

The magician must draw a magic circle and sprinkle upon it the Incense of Abramelin, a mixture of myrrh, cinnamon, olive oil and galingal. He then chants the first part of the conjuration, describing the nature and accomplishments of the spirit to be invoked. This mainly consists of references to pairs of opposites, which are united in the One.

The incantation contains references to Ptah, the Egyptian god of thought, the creator of the world, Ra the sun-god and Khem (Egypt). The magician then moves around the magic circle, pausing at each of the cardinal points to pronounce various Names of Power, the true names of gods, in which the power of the god is contained. At this point, the magician should feel a current of energy coursing through him. He then concentrates upon a mental image of the spirit, placing it directly in front of him.

The magician orders the spirit to bring all other spirits under his control, including those of all the elements, earth, air, fire and water. He then chants more Names of Power, identifying himself with the spirit. 'At the climax,' writes Cavendish in *The Magical Arts*, 'the full force of his magical power gushes from him, he loses all consciousness of his normal self and becomes the mental picture which he only saw before.'

The magician repeats his command for the spirits to be obedient, but this time he does it in the guise of the invoked spirit itself. If he has performed the ritual correctly, the magician should become aware of being filled with light, and hearing his own voice as if from far away.

The Hebrew letter *samekh* was important to Crowley because it corresponds to Temperance in the Tarot, and is the symbol of the soul's passage to a higher plane of experience through orgasm. To the title of the ritual, he added the subtitles 'High Supernatural Black Magic' and 'Intercourse with the Demon', and described it as 'the Ritual employed by the Beast 666 for the Attainment of the Knowledge and Conversation of his Holy Guardian Angel'. According to Crowley: 'It is said among men that the word Hell deriveth from the word "helan", to [hide] or conceal, in the tongue of the Anglo-Saxons. That is, it is the concealed place, which since all things are in thine own self, is the unconscious.' To perform the ritual is thus to liberate the forces of one's own subconscious mind. While performing the ritual, the magician masturbates and chants the Names of Power in a combination of mounting intensity (verbal and sexual), until he reaches a climax in which the physical and the mental are unified, and the power of the magician's subconscious mind is released and channelled towards the realisation of his intentions.

In 1909 Crowley performed, in the company of his pupil and lover Victor Neuburg, one of the pivotal magical operations of his career. It was certainly the most dangerous, and would leave Neuburg a shattered wreck. Crowley himself, according to some, would remain possessed for the rest of his life.

Following a visit to Algiers, the two men travelled south into the heart of the desert, where they intended to conjure the mighty demon Choronzon. The operation required two figures to be drawn upon the sand: one a magic circle that would protect Neuburg; the other the Triangle of Solomon, in which Crowley would perform the ritual. They inscribed the name Choronzon within the triangle, at each point of which they cut a pigeon's throat, sprinkling the blood on to the sand.

Dressed in a black robe and hood, Crowley crouched inside the triangle and allowed the demon to take possession of him. Standing within his own circle, Neuburg called upon the archangels to protect him and chanted an incantation from the dreaded *Grimoire of Honorius*.

Crowley then gazed into the topaz he was holding, and within the depths of the stone he beheld Choronzon. The demon was raging and boasting of his power, claiming to be the origin of all disease and suffering. He then spoke a string of strange and terrible words: *Zazas, Zazas, Nasatanada, Zazas.* According to occult belief, these words form the key that unlocks the Gates of Hell.

As he watched in growing fear, Neuburg became aware of a beautiful woman standing within the triangle where Crowley had been. The woman spoke softly to him, begging him to come to her. But Neuburg retained the presence of mind to realise that she was not a woman, but was really Choronzon attempting to trick him into leaving the protection of his magic circle. With an insane laugh, the demon himself, a fanged atrocity, appeared within Crowley's triangle. Choronzon then attempted to flatter Neuburg, saying that he only wanted to enter the circle so that he might prostrate himself before the man whom he considered his master. Neuburg knew that this was merely another trick, and refused to move an inch.

Choronzon then tried another tactic. He transformed himself into the image of Crowley, lying naked within the triangle and begging Neuburg to bring him water to quench his thirst. Once again, Neuburg refused, and now invoked the Names of God and the Pentagram to subdue the demon and bend him to his will. This had absolutely no effect, and Neuburg, now utterly terrified at the personification of infernal power before him, threatened the demon with all the anger, pain and torments of Hell if he did not obey him.

This, of course, was a rather pitiful threat to make to a demon, and Choronzon said as much. 'Thinkest thou, O fool, that there is any anger and any pain that I am not, or any Hell but this my spirit?'

The infernal creature then assaulted the petrified human with all manner of curses, obscenities and blasphemies. Neuburg had been attempting to keep a record of the magical procedure, and was at this point furiously scribbling Choronzon's words on paper (which must have taken a truly superhuman effort of will). While Neuburg was thus occupied, Choronzon took some sand from the triangle of invocation and threw it on the protective circle, breaking it and allowing him to enter.

The demon immediately threw himself upon the hapless Neuburg and tried to rip out his throat. With death bearing down upon him, Neuburg grabbed a magical knife and, stabbing desperately at the furious demon, screamed the Names of God into the cold night air of the desert. Finally Choronzon was overcome, and retreated to the triangle. As Neuburg frantically repaired his circle, Choronzon again transformed himself into the beautiful woman and made another attempt at seduction. Neuburg, of course, was having none of it, knowing full well what would happen to him if he succumbed to her charms.

All this time, the magical energy of the pigeons' blood had been slowly but steadily diminishing. When it finally ran out, the demon had no choice but to admit defeat and return to the infernal regions from which he had come. He disappeared. The magical operation had been completed.

Crowley later said that throughout he had 'dwelt apart' from the action, and had seen Choronzon appear as a woman, a wise man, a writhing snake and as Crowley himself. He was 'the terror of darkness, and the blindness of night, and the deafness of the adder, and the tastelessness of stale and stagnant water, and the black fire of hatred, and the udders of the Cat of slime; not one thing but many things'.

While occultists accept that some supernatural manifestations may be the result of hallucinations caused by the rigorous preparatory procedures, they also believe that this is not always so. Their reasoning is that, since the worlds of the spirit are fundamentally different from the material world in which we live, they and their denizens cannot be contacted while in a 'normal' state of mind. Although the form in which a spirit appears may well be influenced by the magician's imagination, the spirit itself nevertheless is real. As Cavendish notes:

It may be a force or intelligence that exists independently of the magician, and if so it is no more imaginary than the forces of electricity or gravity, or it may come from within the magician himself, in which case it is no less real than the forces of ambition or pride or desire which we recognise in ourselves.

This naturally leads to the question of whether a mental state should be considered any less 'real' than a physical state.

Upon the outbreak of the First World War, Crowley offered his services to British Intelligence, but was rejected. Angered at this, he sailed for America, where he spent the war years writing anti-British propaganda for the Germans. Although he later claimed that this material was satirical in nature, it did little to endear him to the British press and public. In fact, he became a pariah in his own country, and in 1920 he went to Cefalu in northern Sicily, where he established a temple called the Sacred Abbey of Thelema in a ramshackle farmhouse with his mistress Leah Hirsig (also known as the Scarlet Woman).

Fuelled by opium and cocaine, Crowley and Hirsig (with whom he had a daughter, Poupee) practised occult rites in the company of the few disciples who turned up at the Sacred Abbey of Thelema. It was not long before rumours began to spread of horrific rituals and unspeakable acts performed there. Perhaps the most notorious of these rituals was one in which a goat was said to have been sacrificed while penetrating Leah. Hardly surprisingly, she and the other disciples became increasingly mentally unbalanced, a situation which was not helped by their prodigious use of drugs. Following the death of Poupee in this unsanitary environment, Leah had a nervous breakdown.

The end of the Sacred Abbey of Thelema was brought about by the death of Raoul Loveday, one of Crowley's disciples, apparently from drinking bad water. Shattered by his death (not to mention the other events at the farmhouse), Loveday's widow, Betty May, fled home to England and sold her story to the *Sunday Express*. It seems that the cause of Loveday's death was embellished somewhat, with the impure water becoming the blood of a sacrificed cat. At any rate, the indignant British press went into overdrive, calling Crowley 'the wickedest man in the world'. It was not long before Mussolini's government decided that Crowley had outstayed his welcome, and he was expelled from Sicily in 1923.

In 1925, Crowley was invited to join the magical society known as the Ordo Templi Orientis (the Order of the Temple of the East). The OTO was founded in Germany in the first years of the twentieth century. The Order claimed (and still claims) descent from some of the most famous and illustrious of heretical organisations, including the Bavarian Illuminati, the Rosicrucians, the Albigensians, the Cathars and the Knights Templar.

The Order was created by Carl Kellner (1851–1905) and Theodor Reuss (1855–1923). Kellner was a wealthy Austrian industrialist; Reuss, who became a Mason in 1876, was a journalist and singer, and possibly also a spy for the Prussian secret police. He also attempted to revive the Illuminati, which had been banned a century earlier.

Kellner claimed to have met three Eastern adepts in the 1890s: a Sufi, Soliman ben Aifa, and two Hindus, Bhima Sena Pratapa of Lahore and Sri Mahatma Agamya Paramahamsa. It was at this meeting that Kellner said he had discovered a 'Key' to the mysteries at the heart of esoteric rites. The Key was the sacred application of sexual energy; in other words, sex magic. Kellner suggested to Reuss that they create a Masonic rite for the dissemination of this magical key. The answer seemed to Kellner to be a reformation of the German Hermetic Brotherhood of Light, which had been founded twenty-five years earlier, and whose rites included sexual magic. Initiations into the Order began in 1902; however, the reactions of initiates to the nature of the Key, once revealed, where somewhat ambivalent. Some were shocked by it; others merely found it absurd and left immediately.

Kellner died in early June 1905, leaving Reuss in charge. It was he who chose the name Ordo Templi Orientis – Orientis (east) signifying not only the rising of the Sun, but also the place in which the Key had been discovered. Reuss was known by two magical names: Merlin and Peregrinus. He established the Order's ten-degree structure, although the many rituals he wrote were replaced by Crowley with his own after he joined in 1910.

Reuss chartered several famous occultists to operate OTO lodges in various parts of the world. Rudolf Steiner (1861–1925) opened a German lodge in 1906, and Dr Gerard Encausse (1865–1916) opened one in France in 1908. Dr Arnold Krumm-Heller (1879–1949) opened a lodge to cover the whole of Latin America, although he seems to have done very little to recruit new members, and the Order did not survive there.

Crowley was initiated into the higher mysteries of the OTO following a misunderstanding. In 1912 he published his *Book of Lies*, at which time he was an honorary member of the Order. Reuss read the book, and immediately contacted Crowley, demanding to know what he thought he was doing. With the *Book of Lies* he had revealed to the world the secret of the highest degree of the Order, the Key Kellner had discovered in the East. When Crowley denied the allegation, claiming to have discovered the secret independently, Reuss decided that he would have to be initiated into the Order and immediately sworn to secrecy. On 21 April 1912, Crowley was initiated and given authority over the British Isles.

In 1917 Crowley removed most of the Masonic material from the degrees of the OTO, and replaced it with material relating to his own philosophy of *thelema*, the magical will, with the approval of Reuss, but not of the other lodges. Following Reuss's stroke in the spring of 1920, Crowley became the acting head of the OTO; he proclaimed himself Outer Head of the Order in November of the following year. Reuss died in October 1923.

As we have seen, Crowley's oft-quoted maxim, 'Do what thou wilt shall be the whole of the Law' has been woefully misinterpreted by the uninitiated. Its complement (quoted a little less often) is, 'Love is the Law, Love under Will'. The words 'love' and 'will' (in Greek *agape* and *thelema* respectively) stand at the centre of Crowley's magical doctrine.

In Crowley's case, the maxim 'there's no such thing as bad publicity' was patently false. Hated and feared by the public, unable to find a publisher for his writings and finding himself regarded with horror and disgust almost everywhere he went, he began to wander aimlessly through France (from which he was expelled in 1929), Germany and North Africa among other places, hopelessly addicted to heroin and living precariously off the favours of the few friends he had left. In 1935 he was made bankrupt, having exhausted his inheritance years earlier.

In 1945 he retired to a dingy flat in Hastings, where he died, alone, on 1 December 1947. He had been broken by years of drug abuse, including heroin, cocaine, laudanum and hashish. His reputation as the wickedest man in the world was one in which he revelled at first, but later came to regret, since it stymied so completely his efforts to bring about the New Aeon, an age in which humanity would at last be free of the stranglehold of orthodox religion.

He was certainly the most important magician of the twentieth century, and his legacy has inspired countless musicians, artists and writers. His books are still in print, and continue to attract new devotees every day. Crowley was cremated in Brighton, in a rather bizarre ceremony attended by his friends. His 'Hymn to Pan' was recited in the crematorium, much to the annoyance of the local authorities, who later assured the public that no such incident would ever be allowed to happen again.

EIGHT

Black Magic in
the Third Reich

'The historian may be rational, but history is not.'
LOUIS PAUWELS AND JACQUES BERGIER,
THE MORNING OF THE MAGICIANS

We now turn to an episode in the history of wizardry that has given rise to one of the most controversial claims of the twentieth century. So appalling is this claim that serious historians have consistently dismissed it as the most pernicious kind of nonsense. The claim is simply this: that the horrific nightmare of Nazism and the death and destruction it wrought were the results of an attempt by Adolf Hitler and his minions to contact and enlist the aid of supernatural forces in their bid for world domination. This is a dominant and recurring thread in the history of twentieth-century occultism, and it is essential that we should address it, for it offers a sobering example not only of the pernicious nature of some aspects of occultism, but also of the ways legends can take on a hideous life of their own. Many occultists still believe that those in the highest echelons of Nazi Germany were black magicians. But how accurate is this claim?

The history of the Third Reich inspires a deep fascination among the public to this day, and the ultimate origin of the awful cruelties it perpetrated remains the subject of intense debate. Ever since Hitler committed suicide in Berlin in 1945, historians, psychologists and theologians have tried to understand and explain the reasons behind the horror that was Nazism. Of considerable importance in these attempts is the question of where Hitler stands in the spectrum of human nature. Is he explicable in the same terms that are applied to other mass murderers, occupying the far end of a continuum that includes pacifists and philanthropists at one end, and serial killers at the other? Or is he something else entirely, a monstrous aberration existing outside the continuum of humanity, evil in some absolute, ultimate way?

The theologian Emil Fackenheim believes Hitler's crimes were so extreme that he must be considered as representing a radical evil, an eruption of demonism into history. Thinkers like Fackenheim see Hitler's evil as existing beyond the bounds of human behaviour, transcending the field of behavioural science and entering the realm of theology. In other words, Hitler's nature can, ultimately, be completely understood only by God.

Historians have quite rightly tended to concentrate on the many important economic, social and historical factors that influenced the development of Nazi ideology. However, much less attention has been paid to the Nazis' fascination with esoteric belief systems, a fascination that began in the mid-nineteenth century. Human beings are great myth-makers, and it is hardly surprising that the known history of the Third Reich should have given rise to the belief that the Nazis were, literally, in contact with an evil trans-human intelligence, which succeeded in exerting its influence over human affairs through the magical conduits of Hitler and other high-ranking members of the Third Reich.

The fathers of National Socialism were aggressively anti-Semitic German nationalists who cultivated a profound interest in occultism, theosophy, the idea of Atlantis as a lost Aryan super-civilisation, and the magical powers inherent in the very blood of racially pure Germans. As the Nazis grew more and more powerful, Hitler's own subordinates dabbled in occult sciences such as astrology, and occultism also played a significant role in the formations and rituals of the SS (*Schutzstaffel* or Defence Squads). It is also a matter of historical record that the Nazis embraced bizarre and ridiculous cosmological theories such as Hans Hörbiger's World Ice concept, which provided them with an opportunity to denounce the ideas of the Jewish Albert Einstein.

Many writers on the occult have asserted that the SS was actively engaged in the practice of black magic, and performed magical rites designed to contact and enlist the aid of evil and immensely powerful non-human forces in order to realise the plans of the Third Reich to dominate the planet. While most historians view this idea with contempt, it holds a great attraction for others who are struggling with the dreadful mystery at the heart of Nazism, and who have come to believe that only a supernatural explanation can hope to shed light on the origins and deeds of Nazism. Nicholas Goodrick-Clarke, one of the few serious historians to have explored in detail the occult inspiration behind Nazism, stresses that although the founding fathers of National Socialism (occultists such as Guido von List and Lanz von Liebenfels) undoubtedly contributed to Nazi mythology, with its weird notions of prehistoric Aryan superhumans inhabiting vanished continents, they did not exert a direct influence on people in positions of power.

However, Goodrick-Clarke concedes that there is one exception to this: a man named Karl Maria Wiligut (1866–1946) who greatly influenced Reichsführer-SS Heinrich Himmler. Therefore, before turning our attention to the SS and the magical rites it is alleged to have practised, we will pause to examine the life and thought of Wiligut, and the reasons for his influence over the leader of the most powerful organisation in the Third Reich.

Wiligut was born in Vienna into a military family, and saw action against the Russians in the Carpathians during the First World War. After being transferred to the Italian front, he reached the rank of colonel in 1917, and was decorated for bravery. He was discharged from the army in 1919, after thirty-five years of service. At around this time, rumours began to circulate in Vienna's occult underground that Wiligut possessed an impressive occult talent: an 'ancestral memory' that allowed him to recall the history of the Teutonic people all the way back to the year 228,000 BC. Wiligut himself maintained that this incredible clairvoyant ability was the result of an uninterrupted family lineage extending thousands of years into the past. He claimed that his father had initiated him into the secrets of his family in 1890.

Research conducted by Goodrick-Clarke in the primary sources of the period revealed the origin of this information about Wiligut to be a man named Theodor Czepl, who knew of Wiligut through his occult connections in Vienna, which included Wiligut's cousin, Willy Thaler, and various members of the Order of the New Templars (ONT). Czepl visited Wiligut several times at his Salzburg home in the winter of 1920; during these visits, Wiligut claimed that the Bible had been written in Germany, and that the Germanic god Krist had been appropriated by Christianity.

According to Wiligut's bizarre account of prehistory, the Earth was originally lit by three suns and was inhabited by a variety of fantastic beings, including giants and dwarves. The Earth was ravaged by warfare for tens of thousands of years until Wiligut's ancestors, the Adler-Wiligoten, brought peace with the foundation of the great city of Arual-Jöruvallas (Goslar, the chief shrine of ancient Germany) in 78,000 BC. Conflicts broke out periodically over the next several thousand years involving various now-lost civilisations, until 12,500 BC, when the religion of Krist was established. Three thousand years later, an opposing group of Wotanists challenged this hitherto universal Germanic faith, and crucified the prophet of Krist, Baldur-Chrestos, who nevertheless managed to escape to Asia. The Wotanists destroyed Goslar in 1200 BC, forcing the followers of Krist to establish a new temple at Externsteine, near Detmold.

Wiligut maintained that his own family was the result of a mating between the gods of air and water, and in later centuries fled from persecution at the hands of Charlemagne, first to the

Faroe Islands and then to Russia. His family history was a self-aggrandising mish-mash of genuine cultural traditions (such as those described in the Scandinavian Eddas) and theosophical belief systems that have little or no bearing on the actual history of mythology.

Wiligut claimed that the victimisation of his family had been going on for tens of thousands of years, and was being continued by the Catholic Church, the Freemasons and the Jews, all of whom he blamed for Germany's defeat in the First World War. When his infant son died, bringing the family's male line to an end, his already precarious mental health was further undermined. Wiligut's wife, Malwine, was already singularly unimpressed with his grandiose claims regarding his family's prehistoric greatness, and their son's death placed an even greater strain on their marriage. After becoming increasingly violent and obsessed with the occult, he was committed to the mental asylum at Salzburg in 1924. He was certified insane, and confined there for the next three years.

During his confinement, Wiligut maintained contact with his colleagues in various occult circles, including the ONT and the Edda Society; and five years after his release he decided to move to Germany. He settled in Munich, where he was fêted by German occultists as a source of invaluable information on the remote and glorious history of the German people.

Wiligut's introduction to Heinrich Himmler came about through the former's friend Richard Anders, an officer in the SS. Himmler was greatly impressed with the old man's ancestral memory; SS recruits had to be able to prove their Aryan family history back to the year 1750, but Wiligut seemed to possess an Aryan purity going back very much further than that. Wiligut joined the SS in 1933, and was made head of the Department for Pre- and Early History in the SS Race and Settlement Main Office in Munich. Here, he was charged with the task of writing down the events he clairvoyantly recalled. His work evidently met with Himmler's approval, and the Reichsführer-SS promoted him to SS-Oberführer (Lieutenant-Brigadier) in 1934.

As if his own ravings were not enough, Wiligut introduced Himmler to another occultist, a German crypto-historian named Günther Kirchhoff (1892–1975) who believed in the existence of an ancient grid-work of energy lines crossing the Earth. Wiligut decided to forward a number of Kirchhoff's essays and dissertations on ancient Germanic tradition to Himmler, who ordered the *Ahnenerbe* (the SS Association for Research and Teaching on Heredity) to study them.

However, the *Ahnenerbe* quickly realised that Kirchhoff was a crackpot who understood nothing of scholarly prehistorical research (quite an indictment, coming from that particular organisation). When Kirchhoff accused them, along with the Catholic Church, of conspiring against him, the *Ahnenerbe* responded by describing his work as rubbish and him as nothing more than a fantasist. Nevertheless, Himmler continued to instruct the *Ahnenerbe* to take his rantings seriously, until the outbreak of the Second World War forced him firmly into the background.

Wiligut, on the other hand, made one further contribution to Himmler's SS. While travelling through Westphalia during the Nazi electoral campaign in 1933, Himmler found himself deeply affected by the atmosphere of the region, with its romantic castles and mist-shrouded Teutoburger Forest. He decided to take over a castle for SS use, and in 1934 appropriated the Wewelsburg castle with the intention of turning it into an ideological education college for SS officers. Himmler's view of the Wewelsburg was probably influenced by Wiligut's assertion that it was destined to become a magical strongpoint in a future war between Europe and Asia. Himmler was fascinated by this idea, which corresponded with his own belief that a future conflict between East and West was inevitable. In addition, it was Wiligut who influenced the development of SS ritual and who designed the SS *Totenkopfring* (literally 'Death's Head Ring) that symbolised membership of the order.

In 1935, Wiligut moved to Berlin, where he joined Himmler's Personal Staff and continued to advise the SS on all aspects of his Germanic pseudo-history. The reason for his eventual decision to leave the SS is uncertain, although it may have been because his health had started to deteriorate. He was prescribed powerful drugs to maintain his mental faculties; but these had serious side effects, including personality changes that resulted in heavy smoking and alcohol consumption. His psychological history (including his committal for insanity) also became known, causing Himmler considerable embarrassment. In early 1939, Wiligut's staff was informed that he had retired due to poor health, and that his office would be closed. Although the old occultist was supported by the SS in his final years, his influence on the Third Reich was at an end. After moving house several times throughout the war years, he was finally sent by the British occupying forces at the war's end to a refugee camp where he suffered a stroke. After his release, he went first to his family home at Salzburg, and then to Arolsen, where he died in January 1946.

The man who was so deeply impressed with the rantings of Wiligut, who would become most closely associated with the terror of the SS and an embodiment of evil second only to Adolf Hitler himself, was born in Munich on 7 October 1900. Himmler was not blessed with a robust physical constitution, and this hampered his family's initial intention that he should become a farmer. After serving briefly at the end of the First World War, he joined Hitler's NSDAP (the National Socialist German Workers' Party).

In January 1929, Himmler was appointed head (Reichsführer) of the SS. At that time, the organisation had barely three hundred members, but such were Himmler's organisational skills that he increased its membership to over 50,000 during the next four years. By 1937, the three major concentration camps in Germany were staffed by the SS *Totenkopfverbände* (Death's Head Units), and the following year saw the formation of the *Verfügungstruppe* (Action Groups), which numbered 200,000 and which later became the *Waffen*-SS (Military SS). By the end

of 1938, SS membership had reached nearly 240,000, a figure
that would later rise to approximately one million.

It has been said of Himmler many times that he was a curious
mixture of rationalist and fantasist: that his capacity for rational
planning, the following of orders and administrative detail,
existed alongside an idealistic enthusiasm for utopianism, mysticism and the occult. This combination of the quotidian and the
fantastic led to Himmler's conception of the ultimate role of the
SS: to provide bloodstock for the future Aryan race, and to
become the ideological élite of the expanding Reich.

From 1930, Himmler concentrated on the formulation of his
plans for the SS, which included the establishment of the SS officers' college at the Wewelsburg castle in 1933. Two years later,
he established the *Ahnenerbe* with the Nazi pagan ideologue
Walther Darré. The *Ahnenerbe* was initially an independent institute conducting research into Germanic prehistory, archaeology
and occult mysticism. It was subsequently incorporated into the
SS in April 1940, with its staff holding SS rank. It is likely that
inspiration for the *Ahnenerbe* came from a number of German
intellectuals and occultists who had subscribed to the theories of
an ancient Germanic super race espoused by the nationalist writers of the late nineteenth century, as well as from the adventures
of a number of explorers and archaeologists.

Himmler's vision of the SS required its transformation from
Hitler's personal bodyguard into a pagan religious order with
virtually complete autonomy, answerable only to the Führer
himself. The castle of Wewelsburg was close to Paderborn in
Westphalia, and was close to the gigantic stone monument
known as the Externsteine, where the Teutonic hero Arminius
defeated the Romans.

The principal chamber in the castle was the great dining
hall, with its huge oaken table around which sat twelve of the
senior Gruppenführers – this arrangement owing much to the
legend of King Arthur and the Knights of the Round Table.
Beneath the dining hall was a circular room at the centre of
which was a shallow depression reached by three stone steps

(symbolising the three Reichs). In this place of the dead, the coat of arms of the deceased 'Knight' of the SS would be ceremonially burned. Each member of Himmler's Inner Circle of Twelve had his own room, which was dedicated to an Aryan ancestor. Himmler's own quarters were dedicated to King Heinrich I, the Saxon king who had battled Hungarians and Slavs, and of whom Himmler was convinced he was the reincarnation – although he also claimed to have conversations with Heinrich's ghost at night.

Inside the dining hall, Himmler and his Inner Circle would perform various occult exercises, which included attempts to communicate with the spirits of dead Teutons and efforts to influence the mind of a person in the next room through the concentration of willpower. There was no place for Christianity in the SS, and members were actively encouraged to break with the Church. Christian ceremonies were replaced with new ones; Christmas, for example, was replaced with a specially designed winter solstice ceremony. Weddings and christenings were also replaced with pagan rituals.

As described, the *Ahnenerbe* received its official status within the SS in 1940, and while other occult-orientated groups such as the Freemasons, the Theosophists and the Hermetic Order of the Golden Dawn were being suppressed, the *Ahnenerbe* was given free rein to pursue its own line of mystical and occult enquiry, with the express purpose of providing the historical validity of Nazi paganism. With more than fifty sections, it covered every aspect of occultism and paganism, including Celtic studies, the rituals surrounding the Externsteine monument, Scandinavian mythology, runic symbolism, the World Ice theory of Hans Hörbiger, and an archaeological research group that attempted to prove the geographical ubiquity of the ancient Aryan civilisation. In addition, at the door of the *Ahnenerbe* must lie the ineradicable iniquity of the medical experiments conducted at Dachau and other concentration camps, since it was this organisation that commissioned the hideous programme of 'scientific research' on living human subjects.

The mental ambiguity of Heinrich Himmler – rational, obedient and totally desirous of security on the one hand; immersed in the spurious fantasy of Aryan destiny on the other – was demonstrated most powerfully in the final phase of the Nazi regime, when it became obvious that Germany would lose the war and the 'Thousand-Year Reich' would become dust. From 1943 onward, Himmler maintained loose contacts with the Resistance Movement in Germany, and in the spring of 1945 he entered into secret negotiations with the World Jewish Congress. Himmler's actions at this time indicate what the historian Joachim Fest calls 'an almost incredible divorce from reality', one example being his suggestion to a representative of the World Jewish Congress that 'it is time you Jews and we National Socialists buried the hatchet'. He even assumed, in all seriousness, that he might lead a post-war Germany in an alliance with the West against the Soviet Union. When the reality of the Third Reich's defeat finally overwhelmed his fantasies and sent them to oblivion, and the idea of disguise and escape finally presented itself to him, Himmler adopted perhaps the worst false identity he could have chosen: the uniform of a sergeant major of the Gestapo. He was, of course, arrested on sight.

In the decades since the end of the Second World War, writers on the occult have attempted to explain the terrifying mystery of the true origins of Nazism by attempting to fit it into an occult context. Perhaps unsurprisingly, these writers have paid close attention to an intriguing statement Hitler is known to have made – 'Shall we form a chosen band, made up of those who really know? An order: a brotherhood of the Knights of the Holy Grail of Pure Blood' – and have attempted to use this statement as a point of connection between the Nazis and the occult. Although serious historians such as Nicholas Goodrick-Clarke accept that occult and folkloric concepts played a significant role in the development of Nazi ideas and doctrines, it has been left largely to writers on 'fringe' subjects to push the envelope (wisely or otherwise) and claim that the Nazis were motivated by *genuine* occult forces: in other words, that there exist in the

Universe malign non-human intelligences that seek ways to influence the destiny of humanity for their own ends, and that used the Nazis as conduits through which these influences might work. According to this scheme of history, the Nazis were, quite literally, practising Satanists and black magicians. We have already seen how Nazi ideology was influenced by the ideas of German nationalist occultists in the latter decades of the nineteenth century. But is this as far as the connection goes?

In 1973 Trevor Ravenscroft, a veteran of the Second World War, published a book that caused more controversy than any other dealing with the subject of Nazism, and that is still the subject of heated debate today. Entitled *The Spear of Destiny*, the book chronicles the early career of Hitler, the man who would stain the twentieth century with the blood of millions, and whose name would become a synonym for cruelty of the most repulsive kind. Hailed by some as a classic of occult history and derided by others as no more than a work of lurid fiction, *The Spear of Destiny* is still in print today and, whatever its merits or demerits, remains one of the most important texts in the field of Nazi occultism. (It should be noted that, such is the murky and bizarre nature of this field, to make such a claim for a book is by no means equivalent to defending its historical accuracy.)

Ravenscroft was a commando during the war, and spent four years in German POW camps. He made three escape attempts but was recaptured each time. While imprisoned, Ravenscroft claimed to have experienced a sudden apprehension of higher levels of consciousness, which led him to study the legends of the Holy Grail and the Spear of Longinus. The spear in question was the one said to have been used by the Roman centurion Gaius Cassius to pierce the side of Christ during the crucifixion, the possession of which (so the legend goes) would allow one to hold the destiny of the world in one's hands.

Ravenscroft claimed that, by rights, the man who should have written *The Spear of Destiny* (and would surely have done so, had he not died in 1957) was a Viennese philosopher and wartime British secret agent named Walter Johannes Stein (b. 1891). An

Austrian Jew, Stein had emigrated from Germany to Britain in 1933. His association with Ravenscroft came about as a result of a book Stein had written in 1928 entitled *The Ninth Century: World History in the Light of the Holy Grail*. Ravenscroft was greatly impressed by the book, which asserts that the medieval Grail Romances and their description of the quest for the Holy Grail formed a kind of esoteric map leading to transcendent consciousness (the ultimate goal of wizards throughout history). It was clear to Ravenscroft that Dr Stein had conducted his historical research along rather unorthodox lines, relying on occult methods of mind expansion to apprehend data rather than the more traditional means of consulting extant medieval texts. In view of his own experience of higher levels of consciousness, and his fascination with the Grail legends, Ravenscroft decided to request an interview with Dr Stein.

During their meeting, Ravenscroft voiced his belief that Stein had utilised some transcendent mental faculty in the course of his research for *The Ninth Century*, adding that he believed a similar faculty had inspired Wolfram von Eschenbach to write the great Grail romance *Parsival* around the year 1200. According to Stein, von Eschenbach based *Parsival* on the key figures of the ninth century, who served as models for the characters in the romance. The Grail King Anfortas corresponded to King Charles the Bald, grandson of Charlemagne; Cundrie, the sorceress and messenger of the Grail, was Ricilda the Bad; Parsival himself corresponded to Luitward of Vercelli, the Chancellor of the Frankish Court; and Klingsor, the fantastically evil wizard who lived in the Castle of Wonders, was identified as Landulf II of Capua, who had made a pact with Islam in Arab-occupied Sicily, and whom Ravenscroft calls the most evil figure of the century.

Stein had first read *Parsival* while taking a short, compulsory course on German literature at the University of Vienna. One night, he had a most unusual extrasensory experience in which he recited long sections of the work in a kind of semi-dream state. This happened three times in all. Stein wrote down the words he had been speaking and, on comparing them with von Eschenbach's romance, found them to be virtually identical. To Stein, this strongly implied the existence of some preternatural mental faculty, a kind of higher memory that could be accessed under certain circumstances.

His subsequent researches into the Grail Romances led to his discovery in 1912 in a dingy bookshop in Vienna's old quarter, of a tattered, leather-bound copy of *Parsival* whose pages were covered with annotations in a minute script. Stein bought the book from the shop assistant and took it to Demel's Café in the Kohlmarkt, where he began to pore over its pages. As he read, he grew more and more uneasy at the nature of the annotations, which seemed to have been made by someone who was highly knowledgeable not only on the subject of the Holy Grail, but also on black magic. Stein was repelled yet fascinated by the vulgar racial fanaticism displayed in the annotations, which he regarded as the work of a brilliant but utterly hideous mind, a mind that had inverted the traditional idea of the quest for the Grail as a gradual and immensely difficult awakening to wider spiritual reality, turning it into its antithesis: the opening of the human spirit, through the use of black magic, to the power and influence of Satan himself.

Shaken by what he had read in the pages of the book, Stein glanced up for a moment through the café window and found himself looking into a dishevelled, arrogant face with demoniacal eyes. The apparition was shabbily dressed and was holding several small watercolours that he was trying to sell to passers-by. When Stein left the café late that afternoon, he bought some paintings from the down-and-out painter and hurried home. It was only then that he realised that the signature on the watercolours was the same as that in the copy of *Parsival* he had bought: Adolf Hitler.

According to Ravenscroft, by the time Stein found the annotated copy of *Parsival*, Adolf Hitler had already paid many visits to the Weltliches Schatzkammer Museum (Habsburg Treasure House) in Vienna, which held the Lance of St Maurice (also known as Constantine's Lance), a symbol of the imperial power of the Holy Roman emperors at their coronations. Having failed to gain entry to the Vienna Academy of Fine Arts and the School of Architecture, and growing more and more embittered and consumed with an increasing sense of his own destiny as dominator of the world, Hitler had thrown himself into an intense study of Nordic and Teutonic mythology and folklore, German history, literature and philosophy. While sheltering from the rain in the Treasure House one day, Hitler heard a tour guide explaining to a group of foreign politicians the legend associated with the Lance of St Maurice: that it was actually the spear Gaius Cassius had used to pierce the side of Christ, and that whoever succeeded in understanding its secrets would hold the destiny of the world in his hands for good or evil.

Intent on meeting the man who had written so perceptively and frighteningly in the battered copy of *Parsival*, Stein returned to the dingy bookshop, and this time encountered the owner, an extremely unsavoury-looking man named Ernst Pretzsche, who told him that Hitler pawned many of his books in order to buy food, and redeemed them with money earned from selling his paintings. The shop assistant, he said, had made a mistake in selling the book to Stein. He showed Stein some of Hitler's other books, which included works by Hegel, Nietzsche and Houston S. Chamberlain, the British fascist and advocate of German racial superiority who frequently claimed to be chased by demons.

In the conversation that followed, Pretzsche maintained that he was a master of black magic and had initiated Hitler into the dark arts. After inviting Stein to come and consult him on esoteric matters at any time (which Stein had no intention of doing, such was the loathsomeness of the man), Pretzsche gave him Hitler's address in Meldemannstraße.

Hitler was extremely irate when Stein walked up to him and told him of his interest in the annotations in the copy of *Parsival* he had bought. He cursed Pretzsche for selling one of the books he had pawned. However, once Stein had told him of his own researches into the Holy Grail and the Spear of Longinus, Hitler became more amicable. They decided to pay a visit to the Schatzkammer together to look at the Holy Lance. As they stood before the display, the two men responded to it in very different ways. Stein felt a healing warmth flood his being, as if emanating from the artefact, and filling him with love, humility and compassion. But as he looked across at Hitler, he sensed a hideous and alien euphoria in his companion, who was radiating a wild-eyed evil, as if in the grip of some incredibly malign spirit.

The inscrutable occult processes that were set in motion by Hitler's 'discovery' of the Holy Lance were consolidated twenty-six years later on 14 March 1938, when Hitler arrived in Vienna to complete the *Anschluss* of Austria. While the Viennese people cheered the German forces' arrival, the Jews and opponents of the Nazi regime faced a persecution that, while appalling, was but a pale foreshadowing of the horrors to come. According to Ravenscroft, Hitler went straight to the Habsburg Treasure House to claim the Holy Lance, believing that his bid for world domination was now a very large step closer to being realised.

In spite of the breathless praise that has been heaped upon *The Spear of Destiny* by occult writers over the years, there are many problems with Ravenscroft's account of Hitler's discovery and seizure of the Holy Lance, and also with the very idea of Hitler as a black magician.

We can begin with the lance itself. The existence of a lance that supposedly had been used to stab Christ, is first recorded in the sixth century by the pilgrim St Antonius of Piacenza, who claimed to have seen it in the Mount Zion Basilica in Jerusalem. When the city fell to the Persians in AD 615, the shaft of the lance was captured by the victors, while the lance-head was saved and taken to Constantinople where it was incorporated into an icon and kept in the Santa Sophia Church. More than six centuries later, the point found its way into the possession of the French King Louis and was taken to the Sainte-Chapelle in Paris. The lance-head disappeared (and was possibly destroyed) during the French Revolution. The shaft was sent to Jerusalem in about

AD 670 by the Frankish pilgrim Arculf, and only reappears in history in the late ninth century, turning up in Constantinople. It was captured by the Turks in 1492, who sent it as a gift to Rome. It has remained in St Peter's since then, although its authenticity has never been established beyond doubt.

However, archaeologists have established that this lance, first mentioned in the sixth century, is *not* the one Hitler coveted in the Habsburg Treasure House. This lance, known as the Lance of St Maurice, or Constantine's Lance, was made in the eighth or ninth century.

If *The Spear of Destiny* is to be believed, the moment Hitler entered the Habsburg Treasure House upon the annexation of Austria in 1938 and stood before the holy artefact he had coveted for so long, humanity in the twentieth century was lost, locked on an irrevocable collision course with disaster. And yet there are more problems with this pivotal point in the book. Ravenscroft claims that Hitler triumphantly faced the Viennese crowds on the reviewing stand in front of the Hofburg, whereas Joachim Fest, a great authority on Hitler and the Third Reich, maintains (with photographic evidence to back him up) that Hitler faced the crowds from the balcony of the Hofburg, not from the reviewing stand in front of it.

In addition, Ravenscroft claims that after reviewing the Austrian SS and giving his permission for the founding of a new SS regiment, Hitler refused an invitation for a tour of the city, and also declined to attend the civic dinner and reception in his honour because he was afraid that an attempt would be made on his life. This begs the question: if he was fearful for his life, why did Hitler arrive in Vienna in an open car, and then stand in full view on the balcony of the Hofburg? The claim in *The Spear of Destiny* that Hitler went to the Treasure House on the night of 15 March also presents problems, since records show that Hitler flew out of Vienna late in the afternoon of 15 March: he was not in Vienna that evening.

Historians have frequently returned to Hitler's Vienna period in search of a clue to the origin of his evil. With the story of Stein and the down-and-out Hitler, Ravenscroft also follows this tradition. What makes this story so compelling (regardless of its veracity) is its inclusion of incontrovertible facts about Hitler, juxtaposed with highly controversial material. At this time, he *was* extremely poor, and did scrape a meagre living from selling watercolours to passers-by on the streets. *The Spear of Destiny* treats this period as an incomplete canvass on to which Ravenscroft adds his strange picture of the dark forces motivating the Führer-to-be.

Although it makes fascinating – if lurid – reading, it is not satisfactory as a historical work, and is crippled by the research methods on which Ravenscroft appeared to rely, namely, the use of occult techniques to enhance the powers of the mind and thus gain access to historical information that has not been preserved in any conventional way. In the final analysis, we must dismiss the book on the grounds that when information gathered through psychic processes conflicts with what has been established through documentary evidence or the testimony of first-hand witnesses, we have no serious alternative but to abandon it in favour of what can be verified by those who do not possess these psychic talents.

The history of occultism is inextricably intertwined with the wider history of human affairs. This is just as true of the twentieth century as of any previous period. It is perhaps therefore almost unsurprising that the hideous evil of Nazism should have compelled some to wonder whether the Nazis were practising Satanists and black magicians, and were in contact with malignant supernatural beings. They were not; and so we must accept the terrifying fact that the 'eruption of demonism into history' came not from Hell, but from the uncharted realms of the human mind.

NINE

The Space-Age Wizard

'In these experiences, the ego will be totally altered or completely destroyed in the death that must precede a rebirth into life. The terror, agony and despair that accompany this process cannot be minimized.'

JACK PARSONS, *FREEDOM IS A TWO-EDGED SWORD*

Jack Parsons was one of the founding fathers of American rocket science, a self-educated genius whose development of early rocket propulsion systems helped make NASA's Apollo moon flights possible, and who founded the company that now makes the solid-fuel boosters used on the Space Shuttle. So fundamental was his contribution to space exploration that he has a crater on the moon named after him. He also helped to create the renowned Jet Propulsion Laboratory (JPL) in Pasadena, California, which is at the very forefront of manned and unmanned interplanetary flight. In fact, there is even a joke in the aerospace community that JPL actually stands for 'Jack Parsons Laboratory' or 'Jack Parsons Lives'.

Parsons was a scientific visionary, one of the handful of human beings who believed in humanity's potential as a spacefaring species, and who had the courage and the intelligence not only to see what the future might bring, but to take the necessarily radical and often dangerous steps to realise that future. And the danger was real: in 1952, at the age of thirty-eight, Parsons was killed in a mysterious explosion, the cause of which has never been satisfactorily explained.

He was the epitome of the American pioneer, almost a cliché, in fact. Tall, well-built, ruggedly handsome, irresistible to women, a man who made things happen, he was a living embodiment of the larger-than-life heroes of the pulp science fiction stories he loved so much. Looking at photographs of him, one can easily imagine him at the controls of some outlandish rocketship, with a nubile young assistant at his side, heading for Mars or Venus, or out into the galactic wilderness.

For Jack Parsons, however, rocket science was far from being the whole story: there was another side to his character, another range of interests that consumed him just as fully as chemistry and engineering. In addition to being the all-American pioneer in a brand new science, he was also the practitioner of an ancient one, that of ceremonial magic. In the apparently unlikely setting of 1940s California, Parsons would attempt an occult rite known as the Babalon Working, whereby he would try to summon a powerful and dangerous entity and incarnate it into human form through the impregnation of a female partner. The apparent contradiction of a modern scientist believing so fervently in the power of magic is deliciously ironic and intriguing, and his early life and career give some clues as to the supernatural direction his life would take.

On 2 October 1914, Marvel H. Parsons and his wife Ruth had a baby boy whom they called Marvel Whiteside Parsons. A year later, Ruth divorced her husband on grounds of adultery, and began calling the boy 'John', although she never legally changed his name. Family and close friends would later come to call him 'Jack', while to the scientific community he would be known as 'John'. Parsons would later write that at this time his mother began to cultivate in him an intense hatred for the father he never knew. In his essay 'Analysis By A Master of the Temple', written when he was thirty-four, Parsons wrote (bizarrely, in the second person, that is with reference to himself):

> Your father separated from your mother in order that you
> might grow up with a hatred of authority and a spirit of

revolution necessary to my work. The Oedipus complex was needed to formulate the love of witchcraft, which would lead you into magick, with the influence of your grandfather active to prevent too complete an identification with your mother.

In the absence of his father, the principal male influence in Parsons' early life was his grandfather, Walter. In his fascinating biography of Parsons, *Sex and Rockets*, John Carter speculates that it may have been Walter who encouraged the boy's early interest in fireworks and rockets.

Parsons was a lonely child with few friends; but, as he later wrote, this isolation helped to develop a background of scholarship and love of literature, not to mention contempt for the human herd, which he was to find essential in his adult pursuits. In addition, he developed a powerful hatred of Christianity and what he called its 'guilt sense'.

When he was in the eighth grade at school, Parsons was saved from a bully's attentions by another lad named Edward S. Forman. The two became firm friends, and discovered that they had similar interests, such as the novels of Jules Verne and Hugo Gernsback's newly founded science fiction magazine *Amazing Stories*. They also both loved rockets, and they quickly graduated from setting off fireworks in Parsons' backyard to experimenting with small, solid-fuel projectiles.

In 'Analysis By A Master of the Temple', Parsons wrote:

Early adolescence continued the development of the necessary combinations. The awakening interest in chemistry and science prepared the counterbalance for the coming magical awakening, the means of obtaining prestige and livelihood in the formative period, and the scientific method necessary for my manifestation. The magical fiasco at the age of sixteen was needful to keep you away from magick until you were sufficiently matured.

The exact nature of this 'magical fiasco' is unknown. Around this time, his grandfather passed away, leaving the seventeen-year-old Parsons without a significant father figure and role model in his life. As John Carter notes: 'Most of his adult life [Parsons] sought out others to fulfil this role.'

Parsons and Forman continued to experiment with rockets, often at some risk to life and limb, and in 1932 Parsons went to work for the Hercules Powder Company of Pasadena. The following year he graduated from the private University School and, together with Forman, he attended the University of Southern California. Neither of them graduated.

During their experiments, Parsons and Forman corresponded frequently with other scientists in the field, including Robert Goddard in Roswell, New Mexico (of all places), Willy Ley in Germany (Ley would later flee the Nazis and move to America, bringing with him claims that many Nazis were obsessed with the occult) and Hermann Oberth, the German rocket pioneer. Unfortunately for them, Parsons and Forman eventually realised that their correspondents seemed to be more interested in obtaining information from them than volunteering their own.

In the spring of 1935, Parsons married Helen Northrup, whom he had met at a church dance, and later he wrote, 'The early marriage to Helen served to break your family ties and effect a transference to her, away from a dangerous attachment to your mother.' Around this time, there seems to have been a downturn in the Parsons family's financial situation (until then, the family had been quite wealthy). That autumn, Parsons read an article in the *Pasadena Evening Post* about a lecture given at the California Institute of Technology (Caltech) concerning the rocket experiments of the Austrian Eugen Sänger. The lecture's concluding speculations on the possibility of 'stratospheric passenger carriers' or manned rocket ships reinforced Parsons' belief in the boundless potential of the radical propulsion systems with which he and Forman were experimenting.

The two men were keen to begin experimenting with liquid-fuelled rockets, but lacked the funds to get the project going.

They approached William Bollay, the graduate student who had delivered the lecture on Sänger's work, enquiring about the possibility of working at Caltech – more specifically, at GALCIT, the Guggenheim Aeronautical Laboratory, Caltech – which they hoped would finance their experiments. Bollay was not in a position to offer direct help, but he put them in touch with Frank Malina, who was working on his PhD at Caltech, and who was close to GALCIT's Director, the Hungarian Professor Theodore von Kármán. Malina immediately recognised their talents; although without formal qualifications, they made an excellent team, Parsons the talented chemist, and Forman the expert engineer. Von Kármán agreed to allow the two mavericks to use the GALCIT facilities.

Funds were not quite as plentiful as they had hoped. As Carter notes, at that time 'rockets were still viewed as science fiction by the public. The mere mention of rockets had people thinking of such impossible things as trips to the moon and rarely anything else'. Nevertheless, von Kármán persuaded GALCIT to let Parsons, Forman and Malina use three acres of land, which Caltech leased from the city of Pasadena. The area was called the Arroyo Seco, and lay at the foot of the San Gabriel Mountains behind the Devil's Gate Dam. It is now the site of NASA's Jet Propulsion Laboratory.

The experiments began slowly, mainly due to the shortage of funds from GALCIT; Parsons and Forman had to take jobs to finance the tests they had planned, and to meet their basic living expenses. On one occasion, Malina wrote:

Parsons and I drove all over Los Angeles – looking for high pressure tanks and meters. Didn't have any luck. Two instruments we need costs [sic] $60 a piece and we are trying to find them second hand. I am convinced it is a hopeless task. Will have to approach Kármán.

A few weeks later, the situation hadn't changed.

The early part of this week, Jack Parsons and I covered much of Los Angeles looking for equipment. Our next lead points to Long Beach. Parsons is planning to start manufacturing explosives with another fellow [Forman]. Up to the present time he has been working for an explosives concern. Hope they make a go of it. I have found in Parsons and his wife a pair of good intelligent friends.

In April 1937, Parsons, Malina and Forman left the Arroyo Seco and moved to one of the GALCIT laboratory buildings on the Caltech campus in Pasadena. They had the ever-sympathetic von Kármán to thank. The following month, the group was joined by Hsue-shen Tsien from China. Shortly afterwards, a meteorology student named Weld Arnold presented the group with a small newspaper package. Inside was $1,000 in small bills. No one thought it prudent to ask him how he had come by this impressive amount of cash. In recognition of his contribution, Arnold was appointed unofficial photographer.

The group's time on the Caltech campus did not begin well, as Carter writes in his biography of Parsons:

Campus residents soon resented the group's presence. Testing was loud and violent. Immediately after their arrival on campus, the group met with their first disaster. In the lab they had mounted a rocket motor to a 50-foot pendulum. They measured the swing of the pendulum to calculate the thrust produced. The first motor tested exploded, filling the building with a cloud of methyl alcohol and nitrogen dioxide. A thin layer of rust formed on many pieces of valuable equipment throughout the lab. The other campus residents started referring to the group as 'the Suicide Squad'. Parsons would remember this event four years later, when he finally figured out a way to put the volatility of red fuming nitric acid (RFNA) to good use.

Von Kármán decided that it would be better for the group to move their experiments outside the laboratory. They rebuilt the pendulum, making it five times stronger than was considered necessary, on von Kármán's orders. Two years later, another explosion destroyed the strengthened pendulum, and sent a lump of metal hurtling into a wall where Malina had been standing moments earlier. In spite of his sympathetic attitude to their work, von Kármán decided there was nothing for it but to send them back to the Arroyo Seco.

In spite of these setbacks, the group continued their research undaunted, and were rewarded in the autumn of 1938 when the National Academy of Science (NAS) Committee on Army Air Corps Research expressed an interest in using rockets to assist the takeoff of heavily-laden aircraft. The NAS awarded Caltech a $10,000 contract to develop rocket propulsion with the aim of providing 'super-performance' for propeller-driven aircraft.

The tests that followed resulted in the development in August 1941 of the JATO unit (JATO stands for jet-assisted takeoff, the word 'jet' replacing 'rocket' because of the science fiction connotations of that word). The JATOs had to be used almost immediately; they could not be stored for long periods of time or in extremes of temperature, otherwise they would become unstable and explode. According to Carter, '[Parsons] and Forman would get up very early and prepare the JATOs, nap a little, then meet the others at March Field [the testing site]' and von Kármán wrote, ' [Parsons] used a paper-lined cylinder into which he pressed a black-powder propellant of his own composition in one-inch layers.' In August, the group was ready to test Parsons' JATOs on actual aircraft, the first time this type of rocket had ever been used.

The aircraft they chose for the first test was the Ercoupe, a mail-order hobby aircraft, which was small, light and difficult to stall. The group fitted twelve JATOs under the Ercoupe's wings; each motor delivered 28 lbs of thrust during its 12-second burn. The plane's propeller was removed for the test flight. The pilot, Captain Homer A. Boushey Jr. of the Army Air Corps, took the controls and soared into the air, demonstrating the viability of a propulsion technology that would ultimately take human beings to the moon.

Then, as the 1930s drew to a close, Parsons made a discovery that would, as Carter writes, 'change the direction of [his] personal life as much as Bollay's lecture changed the direction of his professional life'. He was looking through the library of an old friend, Robert Rypinski. The two had met years before, when Rypinski had sold Parsons a used car and Rypinski now worked for JPL. It was among his friend's collection of books that Parsons came across a copy of Aleister Crowley's *Konx Om Pax*, originally published in 1907. The book had proved too complex and abstruse for Rypinski, and so he gave it to Parsons, who almost immediately began to correspond with Crowley. Rypinski later said that to Parsons the book was 'like real water to a thirsty man'.

Aleister Crowley had visited Los Angeles briefly in 1915, and seems to have been singularly unimpressed with the place. It was not until 1935 that Crowley's Ordo Templi Orientis (OTO) had an official representative in the person of an expatriate Englishman named Wilfred Talbot Smith. Hailing from Tonbridge, Kent, Smith had been an associate of Charles Stansfeld Jones (Frater Achad, or Brother Unity), founder of the Agape Lodge in Vancouver, the first OTO lodge on the North American continent. Although Smith had risen to a position of authority within the Agape Lodge, and had met Crowley there in 1915, he fell out of favour and was later expelled. He moved to Los Angeles in 1930 and opened a new Agape Lodge there, which gave weekly performances of Crowley's Gnostic Mass. As Carter explains:

The Gnostic Mass was Crowley's replacement for the 'corrupted' mass celebrated by the Roman Catholic and Eastern Orthodox churches. The text of the Mass, referred to as Liber XV, was written in Moscow in 1913. Partly inspired by the Russian Orthodox Mass, it is surprisingly

Christian in its symbology, and there is nothing obscene about it despite what certain detractors may say. In fact, it is reminiscent of Wagner's *Parsifal* with its repeated references to 'lance' and 'Grail', which are its most suggestive elements. As in the Christian Mass, the Holy Spirit is invoked often. The most openly erotic element in the Mass occurs when the priestess disrobes for part of the ceremony.

In 1939 a scientist colleague of Parsons (whose identity is unknown) took him to Smith's house in Hollywood, where they participated in the Gnostic Mass. Thereafter, Parsons attended regularly with Helen. His meeting with Smith was immensely important to Parsons: not only had he discovered an outlet for his powerful sense of mystery and romance, he had also found the father figure he had lost when his grandfather died.

At this time, the Agape Lodge was run by Smith and his mistress, Regina Kahl, both of whom were extremely authoritarian. In the celebrations of the Gnostic Mass, Smith took the role of Priest and Kahl that of Priestess. Parsons and Helen were initiated into the Lodge on 15 February 1941 and, like many other recruits, they simultaneously became members of Crowley's magical order, the Argenteum Astrum. From the beginning, the handsome and dynamic Parsons made an impression on his fellow members, including the actress Jane Wolfe, who had appeared in several silent films, and who had spent time with Crowley at his Sacred Abbey of Thelema in Sicily. The following is from her *Magical Record*, and was written in December 1940:

Unknown to me, John Whiteside Parsons, a newcomer, began astral travels. This knowledge decided Regina to undertake similar work. All of which I learned after making my own decision. So the time must be propitious ... 26 years of age, 6'2", vital, potentially bisexual at the very least, University of the State of California and Cal Tech., now engaged in Cal Tech chemical laboratories developing 'bigger and better' explosives for Uncle Sam. Travels under sealed orders from the government. Writes poetry – 'sensuous only,' he says. Lover of music, which he seems to know thoroughly. I see him as the real successor of Therion [Crowley]. Passionate; and has made the vilest analyses result in a species of exaltation after the event. Has had mystical experiences, which gave him a sense of equality all round, although he is hierarchical in feeling and in the established order.

Parsons' magical name was Frater T.O.P.A.N. The initials stood for *Thelemum Obtentum Procedero Amoris Nuptiae* ('the obtainment of *thelema* [will] through the nuptials of love'). Helen became Soror Grimaud.

Jane Wolfe's comment regarding Parsons' potential bisexuality is probably inaccurate. Carter notes that this may have occurred to her as a result of Parsons' closeness to Smith, coupled with the fact that Parsons sweated profusely and attempted to mask his strong body odour with heavy cologne. 'A man who wore a lot of cologne at the same time that he displayed an above-average interest in another man may have inadvertently given the impression of bisexuality.'

Whatever Parsons' sexual proclivities may have been, his attitude to sex itself was clear enough. His enormous house at 1003 South Orange Grove Avenue in Pasadena became home to an astonishing variety of free-living and free-loving types, including musicians, artists, writers and anarchists. It was not long before Parsons' strange, eclectic and ever-changing group of tenants became the subject of rumour and lurid speculation in the neighbourhood. There were numerous whisperings of black magic rituals and sexual orgies, and one evening in 1942 several people called the police, claiming that a pregnant woman was jumping naked through a fire in Parsons' back yard. When several officers arrived to investigate, Parsons politely informed them that as a reputable scientist he had no interest in such bizarre silliness. The police officers were convinced, and left without taking the matter further.

In keeping with his scientific and occult interests, Parsons included many science fiction writers among his friends and acquaintances. During the 1940s, science fiction was still in what is known as its 'golden age', and the West Coast boasted a number of key writers. Many of these gathered at Parsons' home, including such SF luminaries as Jack Williamson, A. E. van Vogt, Robert Heinlein, Ray Bradbury and SF historian Forrest J. Ackerman. In addition to being influenced by his reading of science fiction, Parsons seems also to have influenced at least one of these writers: Robert Heinlein used some of Parsons' ideas in what would become one of the most famous of all science fiction novels, *Stranger in a Strange Land*.

L. Ron Hubbard came into Parsons' life in August 1945. The two were introduced while Hubbard was on leave from the Navy, and immediately they found that they had much in common, most notably their interest in science fiction and the mysteries of the occult. Parsons was greatly impressed with Hubbard, and invited him to move into the house on South Orange Grove Avenue. However, it was not long before Hubbard had begun a passionate affair with Parsons' girlfriend, Betty Northrup, who was his wife Helen's younger sister (Helen had already left Parsons for Wilfred Smith). In a letter to Aleister Crowley, Parsons noted that, although he was not a formally trained magician, Hubbard nevertheless possessed an impressive understanding of the subject. Parsons believed that Hubbard was in direct contact with some trans-human intelligence, perhaps his Holy Guardian Angel. He added that he needed a magical partner for the many experiments he was planning.

The most important of these experiments was known as the Babalon Working, by which Parsons hoped to create an elemental being, a supernatural intelligence, the creation of life signifying the magician's power over nature. This operation is far too long and complicated to describe here in its entirety, and so we must limit ourselves to a briefer description. Together with Hubbard, Parsons began the Babalon Working in January 1946, having consecrated his magical equipment, including the Air Dagger, a magical weapon used to provide a focus for occult power and which he had purchased for the purpose. Choosing one of the squares from the Enochian Air Tablet, he copied its magical symbols related to the element of air on to virgin parchment, which consisted of a planetary sign, a zodiacal sign, a certain permutation of the four signs of the elements, and an Enochian letter.

Many who knew Hubbard were of the opinion that he was something of an eccentric confidence trickster, and John Carter makes the interesting point in *Sex and Rockets* that Hubbard's relationship with the good-hearted and diligent Parsons was akin to Edward Kelly's relationship with John Dee (see Chapter Five).

The first task of the working was to trace in the air with the magical dagger the sign of the pentagram. Next, Parsons recited the Invocation of the Bornless One from the grimoire known as the *Lesser Key of Solomon*. After reciting the Third Call, which is designed to summon EXARP, the Angel of the Air Tablet, followed by an Invocation of God, Parsons then invoked the Six Seniors of the Air Tablet, whose names are HABIORO, AAOZX-AIF, HTNMORDA, AHAOZAPI, AVTOTAR and HIPOTGA. Next, he conducted an Invocation of the Wand, in which he fertilised the parchment containing the symbols from the Air Tablet by masturbating over it. When the first part of the working was over, Parsons performed the necessary banishing rituals, including the License to Depart from the *Lesser Key of Solomon*.

While performing this part of the Working, Parsons noted that a powerful windstorm had begun, in keeping with his conjuration of the Angel of the Air Tablet. The wind continued as he performed the invocation again, this time playing Prokofiev's Violin Concerto No. 2 as he did so.

On the night of 10 January, he was awakened at midnight by nine loud knocks. When he got up to investigate, he noticed a lamp that lay smashed on the floor. This was not an intended result of the working, and meant that magical energy had been somehow misdirected. Parsons was an experienced enough magician to realise that something was wrong, but he continued with the Babalon Working anyway. John Carter notes an interesting coincidence here, considering that L. Ron Hubbard was the Scribe: the word HUBARD in Enochian means 'living lamps'.

On 14 January, as Parsons began the working for that day, there was an unexpected power cut. According to Parsons, 'another magician who had been staying in the house and studying with me was carrying a candle across the kitchen when he was struck strongly on the right shoulder, and the candle knocked out of his hand'.

The following day, he wrote that the Scribe had developed a form of astral vision, with which he had described an old enemy of Parsons'. Later in his room, Parsons became aware of a strange, buzzing, metallic voice, which demanded to be allowed to go free. (The 'old enemy' could have been a corrupt police officer, Captain Earle E. Kynette. In May 1938, Parsons had been called as an expert witness in the trial of Kynette, who had been accused of planting a pipe bomb in the car of a vice investigator named Harry Raymond. Parsons' testimony had led to Kynette's conviction for murder, in spite of death threats made against him.)

Parsons performed the License to Depart; however, although the spirit returned to its rightful place, the strange feeling of oppressive tension continued for several days. The only apparent occult manifestation resulting from his efforts thus far had been the windstorm, and Parsons was deeply disappointed with his magical work. However, on 23 February 1946, things had changed very much for the better. He excitedly wrote to Crowley that he had finally found his elemental, in the form of a woman who arrived one evening following the conclusion of the operation. He described her as having red hair and green eyes, just as he had specified in the ritual.

Parsons' 'elemental' was, in fact, Marjorie Elizabeth Cameron, a strong-minded, self-reliant artist who had recently arrived at the Agape Lodge. Although she was unaware of the nature of the Babalon Working, she participated in its next phase, for which Parsons made her a protective talisman. Parsons was more than satisfied with the woman he saw as his elemental, writing of her (as usual, in the second person) that she 'demonstrated the nature of woman to you in such unequivocal terms that you should have no further room for illusion on the subject'.

Parsons and Cameron became inseparable; she became his magical partner, and he educated her in the mysteries of the Occult. In late February, Cameron went back to New York briefly, in order to finish with her boyfriend. When she returned to Pasadena, she discovered that she was pregnant by Parsons, who in the meantime had gone into the Mojave Desert to perform a magical rite the nature of which is unclear, but which resulted in a revelation described in his book *Liber 49*.

In March 1946, the Babalon Working entered its second phase, which included material Parsons had received while in the Mojave Desert. Hubbard, who had been away for several days, returned, saying that he had had a strange vision of a 'savage and beautiful woman riding naked on a great cat-like beast'. He was anxious to impart to Parsons some message, and so they made the necessary magical preparations, constructing an altar and dressing in robes, Hubbard in white and Parsons in black. Hubbard suggested they play Rachmaninov's 'Isle of the Dead' as background music. At 8.00 p.m., Hubbard began to dictate, with Parsons transcribing as he spoke.

The material received represented a triumphant contact with the goddess Babalon, in which she gave them detailed instructions for the next phase of the Babalon Working, which Parsons conducted with Cameron.

As the Working progressed through its many phases, Parsons wrote to Crowley to keep him informed of how it was going. Although Parsons gave the impression that he was well in control of the magical working in which he was engaged, Crowley became concerned, and on 15 March he wrote to Parsons warning him about his relationship with Cameron. Crowley reminded him of the advice given by the great magical theoretician Eliphas Lévi, that a Magus may love his elementals too much, and that this has the potential to destroy him.

Crowley had an accurate suspicion of Parsons' ultimate goal, for he wrote, 'Apparently he, or Hubbard, or somebody, is producing a moonchild. I get fairly frantic when I contemplate the idiocy of these goats.'

With the Babalon Working, Parsons was indeed trying to create a moonchild, an elemental being into whom Babalon would be able to incarnate. It is unlikely, however, that he was attempting to cause a moonchild to be born. As Carter notes, Cameron later claimed that she had become pregnant by Parsons, and had had an abortion with Parsons' agreement. If the couple had been trying to create a moonchild, Cameron would not have aborted her baby. Carter suggests that Parsons was hoping that an adult female would arrive in the same way as had Cameron. In the arrival of the moonchild, Parsons expected and hoped for the arrival of a female messiah, in the form of the incarnated goddess Babalon.

In February 1946, while undertaking the Babalon Working, Parsons formed a company with Hubbard and Betty, called Allied Enterprises. They intended to buy boats on the East Coast, transport them to California and resell them at a profit. Hubbard invested nearly $2,000, Parsons nearly $21,000.

After the Babalon Working had been completed, Hubbard left with Betty and $10,000 of the company's money. The plan had been for them to go to Miami, buy a boat and sail it to California for resale; however, Parsons discovered that they were still in Miami, with no intention of selling the three boats they had bought. He went to Miami and Howard Bond's Yacht Harbour, where he was informed that Hubbard and Betty had taken one of the boats out to sea. Furious, Parsons returned to his hotel room, where he summoned Bartzabel, a warlike spirit associated with Mars, to go after them. When this operation had been completed, Hubbard's vessel was struck by a sudden squall at sea, and only just made it back to Miami in one piece. Parsons then filed a lawsuit against Hubbard, and got two of the boats back, along with a promissory note from Hubbard for nearly

$3,000. Parsons returned to California, but this was the last he ever heard from Hubbard and Betty.

At this time, Parsons was also under investigation by the FBI for several reasons, including his membership in occult groups and his suspected communist sympathies. In addition, the FBI found that while working for Hughes Aircraft, Parsons had taken several research files. Parsons was highly sympathetic to the state of Israel, and it has been suggested that he may have been included in a plan to secure a nuclear weapon for the newly founded state. As a result, Parsons permanently lost his security clearance, and was reduced to working at a gas filling station and occasionally designing explosive special effects for the film industry.

It seems that on Hallowe'en 1948, Babalon returned to Parsons and instructed him to resume his magical activities. This he did by taking the Oath of the Abyss in order to unite himself with the Universal Consciousness through denial of the material world. During the ceremony, he took the magical name Belarion Armiluss Al Dajjal, AntiChrist.

On Tuesday 17 June 1952, Parsons was working on an unknown experiment in his garage. At 5.45 p.m. two explosions ripped through the building. Parsons was killed instantly. There is a great deal of mystery and controversy surrounding his violent end. Some believe the explosion was caused by Parsons dropping a container of fulminate of mercury, although, considering his experience with explosives, this does not seem plausible. Others have suggested that he was murdered by crooked colleagues of Captain Kynette, the corrupt police officer against whom Parsons had testified in 1938. There is also the theory that Parsons was engaged in research regarding the creation of a homonculus, an artificial man said by alchemists to possess magical powers.

The magical records left behind by Parsons have enabled (as was his intention) other occultists to evaluate the work upon which he was engaged, the intention of which was to understand the nature of reality and humanity's place in the Universe.

One of the most bizarre and thought-provoking (not to mention highly debatable) interpretations of Parsons' work was put forward by the British occultist Kenneth Grant. Grant, whom we shall encounter again later, suggests that the Babalon Working was phenomenally successful, although not in the way Parsons anticipated. Noting that the Babalon Working was completed just months before 'the wave of unexplained aerial phenomena now recalled as the Great Flying Saucer Flap', Grant suggests that the effect of the Babalon Working was to open a gateway through which 'something' was able to gain entry to our world. According to Grant and his followers, that something was a race of strange, chaotic beings known as the Great Old Ones. These beings, denizens of the deepest gulfs of intergalactic space, figure prominently in modern occult circles, thanks largely to their creation in the fantasy and science fiction of a man who would achieve not only posthumous world-wide fame as a writer of superb weird tales, but also as the inspiration for many contemporary occultists. That man's name was Howard Phillips Lovecraft.

TEN

The Dreamer

'The most merciful thing in the world, I think, is the inability of the human mind to correlate all its contents. We live on a placid island of ignorance in the midst of black seas of infinity, and it was not meant that we should voyage far.'

H. P. LOVECRAFT, 'THE CALL OF CTHULHU'

It is ironic to say the least that a writer of weird and fantastic stories who had nothing but contempt for occultism and occultists, considering them weak-minded fools or out-and-out charlatans, should have become the inspiration for an entire branch of occult thought and practice. And yet that is precisely what has happened in the case of H. P. Lovecraft, one of the greatest (many would say *the* greatest) and most influential science fiction and horror writers of the twentieth century. Although not a practitioner of the occult himself, Lovecraft has become a central figure in the bizarre world of modern occultism, mainly through his creation of what might be called 'the most famous book never written', the dreaded fictional *Necronomicon* of a mad Arab wizard, Abdul Alhazred. (Usually it is translated as 'The Book of Dead Names', 'Book of the Dead' or 'Book Concerning the Law of the Dead'.) Much to the bemusement and annoyance of serious Lovecraft scholars, many modern practitioners of magic claim that Lovecraft was the unwitting conduit for the transmission of genuine and highly dangerous information from beyond our Universe.

There is an additional irony in the *Necronomicon*'s fame. This non-existent book has become a metaphor for all the forbidden occult knowledge that has been preserved in real magical grimoires over the centuries. The *Necronomicon* has also become a metaphor for the power of the written word itself; however, like the real magical texts of history such as *The Key of Solomon* and the *Grimoire of Honorius*, the essence of the *Necronomicon*'s power lies in what people believe about it, rather than what it contains. Whether real or imaginary, occult texts are seen as inherently dangerous, with the ability to render the human mind vulnerable to inimical forces existing beyond the physical world.

The quotation at the beginning of this chapter, taken from 'The Call of Cthulhu', one of Lovecraft's strangest and finest tales, could easily be applied to the man's life. He intended it as a warning to humanity not to be too anxious to explore the Cosmos, lest we encounter the powerful forces and maddening horrors that surely exist out there in the form of terrifying beings from the unplumbed depths of space and time, who constantly await the opportunity to return to the Earth they once ruled, and obliterate humanity in the process.

Among these terrible beings of Lovecraft's story, known as the Great Old Ones (as well as the Outer Ones or simply the Old Ones) are: Azathoth, the 'monstrous nuclear chaos' that blasphemes and bubbles at the centre of infinity, beyond the realms of angled space; Yog-Sothoth, the 'All-in-One and One-in-All' who is coterminous with all space and time, and appears to those unfortunate enough to encounter him as a 'congeries of iridescent globes' and who is the Gate through which the Great Old Ones will one day re-enter our Universe to wreak their havoc; Shub-Niggurath, the black goat of the woods with a thousand young; Hastur the Unspeakable, 'Him Who is not to be Named'; and, perhaps most memorable of all, the vast, tentacle-headed Cthulhu, the living abnormality that came from the stars when the Earth was young and now lies 'not dead, but dreaming' within the horrible underwater city of R'lyeh, built millions of years before the advent of humanity. Cthulhu's nature is expressed in the strange couplet from the *Necronomicon*:

That is not dead which can eternal lie,
And with strange aeons even death may die.

Occasionally in Lovecraft's stories, a phrase in the language of R'lyeh is presented, which is deeply unsettling in its own right, in spite of (or perhaps because of) the virtual impossibility of correct pronunciation. The most well-known of these snippets of an ancient alien tongue is *Ph'nglui mglw'nafh Cthulhu R'lyeh wgah'nagl fhtagn'*, which translates roughly as 'In his house at R'lyeh dead Cthulhu waits dreaming'. When these beings erupt into our Universe, as they are wont to do from time to time through the activities of certain cultists and those unwise enough to conduct occult research with forbidden books such as the *Necronomicon*, the consequences are invariably dire, for to be in their presence is to know madness and death ...

Tall, gaunt and vaguely cadaverous-looking, and yet possessed of a sensitivity and kindness that gave the lie to his slightly sinister appearance, Lovecraft himself lived (figuratively at least) on a 'placid island' from which he rarely voyaged far. In the picturesque and tranquil setting of Providence, Rhode Island, he created worlds of horror and madness, which included a warped and alien-haunted version of the New England he loved. For his protagonists, knowledge of the true nature of the Universe comes at a heavy price: screaming insanity at best, the complete destruction of body and soul at worst.

Howard Phillips Lovecraft was born on 20 August 1890 in his maternal grandfather's home at 454 Angell Street in Providence. A few months after his birth, Lovecraft's parents returned to their rented home in Dorchester, Massachusetts. His father, Winfield Scott Lovecraft, was a commercial traveller based in the Boston area for Gorham & Co., Silversmiths. In the summer of 1892 the family spent a holiday in Dudley, Massachusetts, and later moved for a while into the Auburndale home of the poet Louise Imogen Guiney, who was a friend of Lovecraft's mother, Sarah Susan Phillips.

It seems that the Lovecraft family would have moved permanently to Massachusetts, had it not been for the sudden deterioration of the father's health. According to S. T. Joshi, the foremost scholar of Lovecraft's life and work, in his *A Subtler Magick*, Winfield suffered a seizure in a Chicago hotel in April 1893, and was brought home in a straitjacket. On 25 April he was admitted to the Butler Hospital, an asylum in Providence. 'The subsequent diagnosis was "paresis", at that time a catch-all term for a variety of neurological diseases, but it is now virtually certain that Winfield had syphilis.' There has been some speculation that Lovecraft himself may have had congenital syphilis, although Joshi states that when Lovecraft was admitted to Jane Brown Memorial Hospital during his own terminal illness in 1937, he was given a Wassermann test, and the result was negative.

Winfield's illness forced Lovecraft and his mother to return to the family home in Providence. It was located on the exclusive East Side of the city, where the wealthiest and most respected families lived. Indeed, the Lovecraft family was itself somewhat illustrious: Sarah was descended from 'old Rhode Island stock – the Phillips family – tracing its roots to the late seventeenth century', while Winfield's family came from Devonshire and settled in upstate New York in the early nineteenth century. In Lovecraft's youth, Providence (and the rest of New England) was largely untouched by the modernity that was encroaching elsewhere. This environment heavily influenced Lovecraft's outlook and opinions: he often stated that he felt like a stranger in his time, and wished that he had been born in the eighteenth century.

His great intelligence was evident from his earliest years: he could speak by the age of one, and was learning Latin by eight. At that time, it was not mandatory for children to attend public school, and so Lovecraft was allowed to explore the large family library in solitude. Here he discovered Grimm's *Fairy Tales* and the *Arabian Nights*, which contributed to his growing love of the exotic and fantastic. The worlds of classical antiquity fascinated him, and broadened his intellectual development considerably, as did the works of the great eighteenth-century poets and essayists. His devotion to fantasy and romance was, however, tempered by his discovery around the age of ten of chemistry, geography and especially astronomy. The resulting sense of scientific rationalism that characterised his intellect led him not only to be contemptuous of professional occultism, but also enabled him to add convincing detail to his later stories. This can be seen most strikingly in the short novel *At the Mountains of Madness* (1931), in which the inclusion of geographical and palaeontological discussion adds an eerie plausibility to an already splendidly macabre science fiction tale.

In 1898 Lovecraft discovered one of his great literary influences, Edgar Allan Poe. As Lovecraft himself later wrote: 'Then I struck EDGAR ALLAN POE!! It was my downfall, and at the age of eight I saw the blue firmament of Argos and Sicily darkened by the miasmal exhalations of the tomb!' Poe was to cast a literary shadow across the rest of Lovecraft's short life, but of perhaps greater importance in shaping his philosophy and the concerns he addressed in his later weird fiction was the science of astronomy. In an essay entitled 'A Confession of Unfaith', written in 1922, Lovecraft states that the discovery of the Hellenic world was of the utmost significance to his intellectual development.

In *A Subtler Magick*, S. T. Joshi notes that by 1904, 'much had happened in Lovecraft's personal life'. Following his father's illness, his maternal grandmother died in 1896, and the boy became extremely frightened by the mourning clothes of the women in his family. According to Joshi, it was at this time that Lovecraft's 'career as a great dreamer' began, for he was plagued by terrifying dreams in which horrific creatures called 'nightgaunts' seized him by the stomach and carried him off on bizarre cosmic voyages. He would later incorporate this idea into his weird fiction: the night-gaunts became among the strangest and most sinister of his creations, carrying the unwary to the dreadful Vale of Pnath, where an unthinkable fate awaited them. In fact, many of his stories were inspired by the nightmares he suffered throughout his life. This curious fact is of extreme importance to the many occultists who are fascinated by his work, for they claim that it was through his nightmares that Lovecraft made unwitting contact with the realms of the Outer Darkness, the vast gulfs stretching beyond the sane and ordered Universe of space and time. The only way he could give voice to the shuddersome information he obtained during sleep was through the writing of his *outré* stories.

With his own father in a mental asylum, the role of intellectual mentor to the young Lovecraft was assumed by his maternal grandfather, Whipple Van Buren Phillips, a wealthy industrialist who offered constant encouragement to Lovecraft in his writing. His elder aunt, Lillian D. Phillips, married Dr Franklin Chase Clark in 1902. Clark was a classicist who had translated Homer and Lucretius, and he contributed greatly to Lovecraft's classical studies.

During his high school period, Lovecraft wrote two stories, 'The Beast in the Cave' (1905) and 'The Alchemist' (1908), but then abandoned fiction in favour of scientific writing and poetry. Although many mistakenly believe him to have been a lifelong recluse, in the period following high school Lovecraft did indeed withdraw completely from society, reading voraciously in all manner of fields, including the cheap pulp literature of the time. Notable on his reading list were the Munsey magazines, which included *Argosy* and *All-Story*. The trite love stories of a writer named Fred Jackson prompted Lovecraft to write a scathing letter, which was published in the September 1913 issue of *Argosy*. This elicited an equally angry response from Jackson's supporters, including a John Russell, who criticised Lovecraft in a poem. Lovecraft responded with his own satirical verse, and the literary spat continued for several months, until finally the editor of *Argosy* decided enough was enough and asked Lovecraft and Russell to abandon their hostilities. This they did, and metaphorically shook hands by composing a poem together, which was published in the October 1914 issue.

What seemed initially like a minor controversy among the devotees of popular literature was to have profound and positive consequences for Lovecraft as a writer. The Jackson correspondence came to the attention of Edward F. Daas, official editor of the United Amateur Press Association (UAPA), who invited both Lovecraft and Russell to join. Lovecraft did so in April 1914, Russell a year later.

The amateur press turned out to be the perfect outlet for Lovecraft, who was able to shake off his reclusiveness and ultimately find an enthusiastic audience for his literary endeavours. As Lovecraft himself stated in 1921:

> In 1914, when the kindly hand of amateurdom was first extended to me, I was as close to the state of vegetation as any animal well can be ... With the advent of the United I obtained a renewed will to live; a renewed sense of existence as other than a superfluous weight; and found a sphere in which I could feel that my efforts were not wholly futile. For the first time I could imagine that my clumsy gropings after art were a little more than faint cries lost in the unlistening void.

So taken was he with the amateur press that Lovecraft even allowed his two earlier tales, 'The Beast in the Cave' and 'The Alchemist' to be published in amateur journals. Pleasantly surprised at the enthusiastic response, he decided to begin writing fiction again, the first results being 'The Tomb' and 'Dagon', both written in the summer of 1917. However, it was not until two years later, when he discovered the work of the great fantasist Lord Dunsany, that Lovecraft finally threw himself headlong into fiction writing.

On 24 May 1921, Lovecraft's mother died. She had spent the last two years of her life at Butler Hospital following a nervous breakdown. Joshi suggests that this event, while obviously tragic, was also a 'liberating influence' for Lovecraft. Given her highly ambivalent feelings towards her son, with whom she had shared the house on Angell Street from 1904 to 1919, this is not as harsh a statement as it sounds. Susan Lovecraft's gradually worsening mental illness caused her to become disoriented in public, and to believe that she could see strange creatures watching the family home. She also informed acquaintances that her son did not like to leave the house because of his 'hideous' face. (Although no matinée idol, Lovecraft was far from hideous.) It is likely that her horror and embarrassment at the awful manner of her husband's death was the cause of her love-hate attitude to her son, in addition to her vehement disapproval of his association with the amateur press.

Although initially devastated by his mother's death, Lovecraft recovered quickly, and his physical and mental health improved dramatically after the age of thirty. It was at this time that he began to travel throughout New England, frequently with friends who were amazed at his new-found energy and vitality.

While attending the NAPA's national convention in Boston in the first week of July 1921, Lovecraft met Sonia Haft Greene, a Russian Jewish widow who was ten years his senior. Although racially prejudiced, Lovecraft was nevertheless captivated by her charm and intelligence. After a three-year courtship, they married and settled in Sonia's large apartment in Brooklyn, New York. However, financial misfortune befell them almost immediately. The hat shop Sonia managed went bankrupt, cutting off all income for the household. Lovecraft searched for work with the utmost effort, attempting to secure employment in all manner of fields, all without success. Lovecraft's problem was that his fragile emotional and physical constitution was singularly unsuited to New York life, and his failure to bring in money for himself and Sonia only exacerbated the trauma. In addition, he had never had a steady job in his life, and so had no professional track record to offer any prospective employer.

The couple's financial pressures soon took their toll on Sonia, whose own health began to suffer. Eventually, she found a job at a department store in Cleveland, Ohio. This, of course, meant that she had to relocate there, while Lovecraft stayed in New York. They could not afford to keep the apartment in Brooklyn, and so on New Year's Eve 1924, Lovecraft moved into a decrepit one-room flat on Clinton Street in Brooklyn Heights. His new home was a dreadful place populated by extremely unpleasant types. A few months after he moved in, his flat was burgled, and he was left only with the clothes he was wearing. Although he had a number of friends and acquaintances in New York, whom he had met through his activities in the amateur press, he became so ashamed and depressed by his situation that he could not bring himself to see them.

A year of this misery was about all Lovecraft could stand, and late in 1925 he wrote home to his two aunts that he wished to return to his beloved Providence. This he did on 17 April 1926. In his book *Lovecraft: A Study in the Fantastic*, Maurice Lévy notes the great significance of this homecoming, which was spiritual as well as physical. He felt settled once again in the familiar surroundings he loved, and was no longer distracted by the sexual responsibilities of a husband.

Lovecraft made it clear to Sonia that he could never bring himself to leave Providence again. She responded with the suggestion that she join him there, buying a house in which the couple and Lovecraft's two doting aunts could live together, and using part of it for a new business venture. However, his aunts informed her, gently but in no uncertain terms, that the family could not afford to have Lovecraft's wife work for a living in Providence; the damage to their social reputation would simply be too great.

It was clear to everyone that the marriage could not continue under these circumstances, and divorce proceedings were undertaken in 1929. Lovecraft returned with some relief to his bachelor existence, spending all his time reading, writing and travelling throughout New England, but also as far north as Quebec and as far south as Key West. The pitiable state of his finances compelled him to travel by bus at night, in order to avoid the expense of staying in hotels; and when it was necessary to find overnight accommodation, he stayed in YMCAs.

In this way Lovecraft spent the final eleven years of his life. When at home, he would work either through the night or during the day with the curtains drawn and the lights on, pretending it was night. With a certain pride he subsisted on as little as $1.75 per week, which he spent on canned beans and spaghetti, crackers, ice cream and sweets. As Lévy notes, this diet could hardly have been good for his already precarious health. With his aunts, Lillian Clark and Annie Phillips Gamwell, constantly watching over him, he quietly produced the astonishing stories and short novels for which he has achieved posthumous worldwide fame. Among the most important of these are 'The Call of Cthulhu' (1926), *The Dream-Quest of Unknown Kadath* (1926–27), *The Case of Charles Dexter Ward* (1927), 'The Colour Out of Space' (1927), 'The Dunwich Horror' (1928), 'The Whisperer in Darkness' (1930), *At the Mountains of Madness* (1931), 'The Shadow Over Innsmouth' (1931) and 'The Shadow Out of Time' (1934–35). In addition, he wrote long travelogues of his journeys to 'antiquarian oases' (Joshi) such as Philadelphia, Richmond, Charleston and New Orleans, as well as a truly staggering number of letters to his friends and colleagues in the amateur press.

In spite of his many excursions, Lovecraft continued to live within himself and his dreams; indeed, his journeys can be seen as an attempt to experience, if only vicariously, a past that was now lost, washed away in the first decades of a century he loathed for its uncouth modernism. Lovecraft hated the reality in which he was forced by chance to live, and took refuge in the outlandish worlds of cosmic mystery he created.

His personal philosophy, expressed so unforgettably through his major fiction, was what he termed 'cosmicism', or mechanistic materialism, which developed out of his early fascination with physics, chemistry and astronomy. There is no room for God in Lovecraft's view of the universe, which he sees as being blindly mechanical and purely material, with no spiritual aspect whatsoever. In his worldview, humanity is not only demoted from primary importance in creation, it is reduced to virtually total insignificance. In this respect, Lovecraft's stories are not, strictly speaking, 'occult'. The monstrous beings spoken of and frequently encountered by Lovecraft's unfortunate protagonists (Azathoth, Yog-Sothoth, Nyarlathotep, Cthulhu and so on) are not gods or demons, but rather immensely powerful extraterrestrial beings. As Joshi notes, it is not even accurate to say that they are hostile to humanity: human beings are destroyed almost by accident, 'as we might heedlessly destroy ants underfoot' as the Great Old Ones follow their own unfathomable agendas. Along with other serious students of Lovecraft, Joshi maintains that these horrifying entities should be seen as allegorical, as symbols for the incomprehensible mysteries of the Universe. The numerous occultists who believe in the literal reality of the Great Old Ones are, according to Lovecraft scholars, making a grievous mistake based on a total misunderstanding of what Lovecraft was trying to achieve artistically. And yet, as we shall see shortly, interest in the Lovecraft Mythos as a genuine and workable magical system is extremely widespread in occult circles.

It is to Lovecraft's great credit as a writer of science fiction that his alien beings are, for the most part, utterly incomprehensible in terms of their nature and motivations, and this is surely one of the reasons for his enduring appeal. The idea that extraterrestrials would bear the slightest resemblance to human beings, either in appearance or psychology, was considered absurd by Lovecraft. For him, the humanoid aliens that were already standard fare in the pulp magazines of the twenties and thirties represented a lamentable paucity of imagination (and it is equally lamentable that such tiresome entities are still present in modern science fiction, particularly in television and film).

Lovecraft was utterly contemptuous of any belief in the significance of humanity in the Universe; his stories expressed a philosophy that was utterly non-anthropocentric in outlook. None of the laws, ethics or emotions that characterise our lonely species has any bearing whatsoever on events occurring in the far reaches of the cosmos. The very idea that an extraterrestrial entity could have anything in common with a human being (including the notions of love and hate, good and evil) struck Lovecraft as puerile in the extreme.

This literary philosophy is best expressed in his own favourite story, 'The Colour Out of Space'. In this truly frightening tale, a meteorite crashes on the farm of the Gardner family in the Massachusetts countryside west of the fictional town of Arkham. The meteorite contains an entity from deep space, a life form so strange, so *alien*, that its very presence causes everything in the area (including people) to crumble gradually to a grey dust. It has other effects, too; effects which are more subtle, yet more terrifying. In one scene, a character called Ammi is driving his horse-drawn sleigh past the Gardner farm:

> There had been a moon, and a rabbit had run across the road, and the leaps of the rabbit were longer than either Ammi or his horse liked. The latter, indeed, had almost run away when brought up by a firm rein.

Truly, as the head of the family Nahum Gardner says, just before his own leached and desiccated body finally succumbs to the effects of the alien presence, 'it come from some place whar things ain't as they is here'. In fact, we know nothing of the physical properties (apart from its colour, which is like nothing seen before on Earth – 'it was only by analogy that they called it colour at all') or motivations of the entity inside the meteorite. It is certainly destructive, but we do not know enough about it even to call it 'evil', or even to say that it is 'alive'. As Joshi rightly states: 'It is the utterly baffling nature of the meteorite and its [inhabitant] – who may not be conscious, organic, or even alive in any sense we recognize – that produces the deeply metaphysical horror in "The Colour Out of Space".'

In 1924, Lovecraft was offered the editorship of *Weird Tales*, which he turned down. Some commentators have suggested that this was a serious professional mistake on his part, stating that his disinclination to make the necessary move to Chicago was not a good enough reason to decline the opportunity of a steady income, of which he was in dire need. However, Lovecraft was aware that the magazine's owner, J. C. Henneberger, was in debt to the tune of $40,000, and its future was in serious doubt.

Instead he turned his talents to literary revision and ghost writing, although the rates he charged were too low to provide a sufficient income, and the long hours he conscientiously put into this activity left him little time to work on his own original material. In 1928 Lovecraft and Frank Belknap Long advertised their services in *Weird Tales*, as a result of which Lovecraft ghostwrote several tales (notably for Zealia Bishop and Hazel Heald), which critics rank among his better efforts.

Towards the end of his life, he devoted more and more time and energy to his correspondence with other writers of fantasy and weird fiction, including Clark Ashton Smith, August Derleth (who would later found the Arkham House publishing company to preserve his friend's work in hard cover after his death) and Robert E. Howard, creator of Conan the Cimmerian. He also helped a great many younger writers, many of whom would go on to achieve worldwide fame, including Robert Bloch, Fritz Leiber and James Blish.

H. P. Lovecraft died on 15 March 1937 in Jane Brown Memorial Hospital of cancer of the intestine and renal failure. It is likely that the disease first manifested around 1934, with Lovecraft passing off the attacks as indigestion. He did not seek medical treatment, certainly because he could not afford it, and perhaps also (as Joshi suggests) because 'he feared a fate similar to that of his mother, whose death was caused by complications following a gall bladder operation'. His very poor diet of canned foods and sweets doubtless also contributed. He was laid in the Phillips family plot at Swan Point Cemetery on 18 March.

The stories on which Lovecraft's reputation chiefly rests have been referred to collectively as his 'Cthulhu Mythos' tales, although the phrase was not invented by Lovecraft, but rather by August Derleth following his death. However, many critics, including Joshi, dislike this phrase, preferring 'Lovecraft Mythos' to describe the worlds and entities he created. (Joshi himself has wondered whether it is even necessary to distinguish these stories from his wider body of work.) As we have noted, these tales are set in a Universe that is far stranger, more dangerous and more terrifying than we can possibly imagine; a Universe that was once ruled, in the unthinkably distant past, by vast and monstrous beings, the Great Old Ones. Some of these titanic beings came from distant galaxies in the far reaches of space, some from other dimensions entirely. All follow incomprehensible agendas in which humanity does not figure at all, save as an infestation on the Earth to be annihilated when the Great Old Ones return to reclaim their property, 'when the stars are right'.

Certain modern occultists have devoted themselves to the principal entities in this bizarre and horrific pantheon, maintaining that they are far more than mere literary inventions. First among these denizens of the Outside is Azathoth, the blind idiot god, whose frightful aspect Lovecraft describes as a gibbering monstrosity, the essence of confusion and madness living beyond the boundaries of the ordered Universe. This 'daemon-sultan' is surrounded by the colossal 'ultimate gods' who dance awkwardly around his throne to the sound of mad drums and whining flutes.

The faithful messenger of the Old Ones, Nyarlathotep goes under a number of epithets, including the Crawling Chaos, the Dweller in Darkness and the Howler in the Night. He can also take on various forms: in *The Dream-Quest of Unknown Kadath*, he appears to the protagonist Randolph Carter as a beautiful young man, while in 'The Haunter of the Dark' he appears altogether more unpleasantly as a black bat-like entity with a single, huge, three-lobed eye. He is worshipped and summoned on Earth by means of a mysterious object called the Shining Trapezohedron, which predates humanity. The Trapezohedron was fashioned on the planet Yuggoth, which astronomers know as Pluto (Lovecraft having ingeniously incorporated the planet into his mythology following its discovery in 1930).

Comparable in power to Azathoth is Yog-Sothoth, who is worshipped by cultists on Earth, and by the vastly intelligent crustacean-like entities of the planet Yuggoth. Lovecraft describes this entity as being coterminous with all space and time, as being the gate through which the Great Old Ones will one day return to claim the Earth and annihilate humanity.

Most famous of the Great Old Ones is the gigantic and quintessentially violent entity Cthulhu, who came to Earth millions of years ago from the depths of interstellar space. In terms of his physical form, Cthulhu is the most closely anthropomorphic of the pantheon, although in truth it is only a passing resemblance. While his scaly body is roughly humanoid, his head is shaped like an octopus or squid, and is dominated by a mass of writhing tentacles; from his back sprout a pair of vast, leathery wings. Following their arrival on Earth, Cthulhu and his spawn built the loathsome city of R'lyeh in what is now the Pacific Ocean. During their heyday, these beings shared the planet with other extraterrestrial beings known as the Elder Things, who built the vast, cyclopean city in Antarctica discovered by the protagonists in the short novel *At the Mountains of Madness*. Due to some unknown antediluvian catastrophe, R'lyeh sank into the sea, imprisoning Cthulhu and his minions within its titanic walls, where they repose to this day, as we have said, 'not dead, but dreaming'. They are worshipped not only by degenerate cultists on land, but by a race of odious beings known as the Deep Ones who live in the lost cities that dot the ocean floors throughout the world.

Very occasionally, through some happenstance of geology or astrology, R'lyeh rises from the ocean depths with horrific consequences, as in 'The Call of Cthulhu'. In this story a group of sailors discover and explore an island that has been thrown up from the depths through seismic activity. What they find in the foul and seaweed-strung corpse-city of R'lyeh is screaming insanity itself. Overcome with fearful curiosity, the sailors manage to open a gigantic door set in a 'grotesque stone moulding', unleashing the abomination. At the appearance of Cthulhu, two of the sailors immediately die of fright.

Cthulhu then pursues them into the sea. Upon reaching the ship, *Alert*, the captain, who is named Johansen, realises that they will not be able to outrun the monster until they get up a full head of steam, and takes the desperate gamble of turning the ship towards Cthulhu and ramming him head on. The prow of the ship bursts open Cthulhu's head. There is a foul explosion of fetid slime, accompanied by an indescribable stench; but then the monstrosity regenerates into its original form as the ship makes its escape. Mercifully for life on Earth, the island and its terrible denizen sink again to the bottom of the sea, to await the time when freedom will be permanent, when the stars become right and the Great Old Ones and all their minions return to claim what is theirs.

Throughout his tales of the Great Old Ones and the hapless humans who encounter them, Lovecraft makes reference to certain forbidden manuscripts and books of occult lore. It is in these that his protagonists find the information and clues necessary to the completion of their dubious and ill-advised quests. As we have already seen, the understanding of the Universe and our place within it that they seek is a poisoned chalice to say the least.

Among these blasphemous, abnormal tomes are Ludvig Prinn's *De Vermis Mysteriis*, the *Liber Damnatus* and the pre-human *Pnakotic Manuscripts*. As the pseudo-mythology of the Great Old Ones developed, other writers in Lovecraft's circle contributed to it with their own tales, adding other worm-eaten tomes to the nefarious list. Clark Ashton Smith created the *Book of Eibon*, penned by the Hyperborean sorcerer of that name; Robert Bloch created the *Cultes des Goules* of the Comte d'Erlette; and Robert E. Howard created the *Unaussprechlichen Kulten* of von Junzt. Within their pages can be found secrets too terrible for the eye of mortal humanity, telling of events that

happened on Earth aeons before the first proto-humans sham-
bled across the African savannahs in their blissful stupidity; of
frightful civilisations existing on distant planets and in other
dimensions; of the chaotic beings who strode godlike across the
intergalactic spaces of the primeval Universe.

Among these books, one stands out as particularly blasphemous and vile, achieving infamous fame in Lovecraft's world, in
the world of fantastic literature, and in the wider world of
occultism and black magic: the *Necronomicon*. In response to
the many letters he received from friends and colleagues,
Lovecraft, with his tongue firmly in his cheek, provided a short
essay on the history of the dreaded book. Written in 1927, the
'History of the *Necronomicon*' maintains that the book's original
title was *Al Azif*, the Arabic word *azif* referring to the nocturnal
sounds made by insects, which the Arabs attributed to the howl-
ing of demons. According to Lovecraft's amusing pseudo-
history, the book was composed by one Abdul Alhazred, a mad
poet and wizard of Sanaá in Yemen, who lived during the period
of the Ommiade caliphs around AD 700.

Alhazred, said Lovecraft, was a wanderer, a seeker after
forbidden knowledge, whose curiosity led him from the ruins of
Babylon to the subterranean vaults beneath Memphis; from
Irem, the fabulous City of Pillars, to the ruins of a nameless
town, beneath which he discovered the records of a long-
vanished pre-human race. He spent ten years alone in the great
southern desert of Arabia, the *Roba el Khaliyeh* or 'Empty
Space', said to be inhabited by demons and horrific monsters,
where he learned many appalling secrets of the Universe. He
spent his final years in Damascus, where he composed the
Necronomicon, a dark testament of what he had learned on his
travels. He is said by his twelfth-century biographer Ebn
Khallikan to have suffered a particularly awful death: in the
middle of a crowded market place, he was seized by an invisible
monster and eaten alive.

In AD 950, the *Azif* was secretly translated into Greek
by Theodorus Philetas of Constantinople under the title

Necronomicon. For the next century, those fortunate (or unfortunate) enough to have access to a copy experimented with the incantations contained within its blasphemous pages, with disastrous results. It was finally suppressed and burnt by the patriarch Michael. However, Olaus Wormius made a Latin translation in the late Middle Ages, and his text was printed twice, once in the fifteenth century in Germany, and once in Spain in the seventeenth. It was banned by Pope Gregory IX in 1232, and the Arabic original was lost. Some Latin texts were said to exist, Lovecraft informed his readers, in the British Museum, the Bibliothèque Nationale in Paris, the Widener Library at Harvard, the library at the University of Beunos Aires and in the library of Lovecraft's fictional Miskatonic University at Arkham, Massachusetts. These copies were kept securely under lock and key, not only because they were so fantastically valuable, but also because reading the book could lead to serious mental problems.

Lovecraft's invented history of his blasphemous tome was convincing enough to prompt many readers to write to him enquiring as to whether it really did exist. (And since his death, libraries throughout the world have received similar enquiries from people wishing to consult a copy.) That the book is indeed his invention is placed beyond all serious doubt by the many letters he wrote to readers to disabuse them of the notion that the *Necronomicon* was real. It certainly amused and gratified Lovecraft that his literary endeavours were seen to possess such an air of verisimilitude, although he invariably and conscientiously took pains to point out that what he wrote was *fiction*.

It is a dubious kind of tribute to the power of Lovecraft's vision that, over the years, a number of books have been published purporting to be the real *Necronomicon*, discovered at last after painstaking and dangerous research (and, as the title of a story by science fiction writer John Brunner wryly has it, published in inexpensive paperback editions). Before going on to examine the influence the Lovecraft Mythos has had on certain occult circles, it's worth taking a look at the three most elaborate and best known of these hoax *Necronomicons*. (There are many more fake *Necronomicons* out there, but to deal with them all would require a book in itself.)

The first is known as the 'De Camp–Scithers *Necronomicon*', and it is certainly the most light-hearted of the three. In fact, it is something of a 'ripping yarn', and would not have been out of place in the pages of *Weird Tales*. In his introduction to *Al Azif*, published by Owlswick Press in 1973, the fantasist and Lovecraft biographer L. Sprague de Camp relates how, during a visit to Iraq in 1967 with the science fiction writer Alan Nourse, he stopped in Baghdad to visit the ruins of Babylon and Ctesiphon. De Camp was gathering materials for a book on ancient cities. While shopping for antiques, he was approached by a member of the Iraqi Directorate General of Antiquities, with whom he had previously corresponded regarding photographs of archaeological sites. The man said he had a manuscript he wished to sell, which immediately struck de Camp as odd, since the Iraqi government usually took a dim view of those wishing to export valuable archaeological materials. Nevertheless, he bought it, and gave the matter no more thought until he reached Beirut on his way home.

While in Beirut, de Camp was contacted by a friend of his, a tourist guide who, through his 'many connections throughout the Islamic world', had heard about de Camp's unusual purchase. The tourist guide (whom de Camp of course does not name) claimed that the sale of the manuscript had been authorised 'on a high level of the Directorate General'. It had been unearthed in the tombs of Duria and, 'by devious routes', had found its way into the possession of the Directorate General of Antiquities. The respected archaeologist Ja'afar Babili had been asked to translate the Duriac script into modern Arabic. Barely had he begun this task when he excitedly announced that the manuscript was in fact the *Kitab Al Azif* – the *Necronomicon*. (*Kitab* simply means 'book'.)

As his work continued, Babili noted that the quality of the script deteriorated markedly towards the end of the manuscript, 'as if the scribe were working in haste or under severe pressure'.

A few weeks later, Babili disappeared. No trace of him was ever found, and no plausible reason for his disappearance was forthcoming: he had been conscientious, hard-working and devoted to his family.

The translation work on the *Necronomicon* was turned over to Babili's subordinate, Ahmad ibn-Yahya, who lived in a modest apartment on the Musa al-Kadhim. Two weeks later, his landlady claimed to have heard screams coming from his rooms. When she entered the apartment with her pass key, she found it deserted. Ahmad ibn-Yahya was never seen again.

At this stage, the members of the Directorate General of Antiquities were reluctant to continue work on the manuscript. Eventually, Professor Yuni Abdalmajid of the University of Baghdad agreed to take over. When he failed to appear for his classes, the police were called, and went to his house in the Kadhmiyya District on the outskirts of Baghdad. Upon entering the professor's study, the police discovered spatters of blood on the floor, walls and ceiling, but of the man himself there was no trace.

Had these three scholars suffered the same horrifying fate as Abdul Alhazred? Had they been devoured alive by some cosmic monstrosity that had been somehow awakened and summoned by their reading of the frightful manuscript? De Camp suggests as much in his introduction, wondering whether during their attempts to translate the manuscript, they might have 'unconsciously subvocalized' the passages, thus unwittingly performing the invocations of the entities from Outside. At any rate, the Directorate General was in a quandary: they could not afford to lose any more scholars. It was at this point that the head of the Directorate, the violently anti-American Dr Mahmoud ash-Shammari, came up with a fiendish scheme. He would arrange for the manuscript to be smuggled into American hands, where it would doubtless wreak all manner of supernatural havoc.

Having told him of the manuscript's true nature, de Camp's friend advised him to destroy it without delay. De Camp scoffed at the notion: he was, after all, well known as a rationalist with no belief in the reality of the supernatural. Nevertheless, he returned home 'with the sensation of travelling with a ticking package in my gear'. After pondering the question of what to do with the manuscript, he decided to publish it in facsimile, with a warning to his readers not to attempt a translation.

This, then, is de Camp's account of how he came into possession of the fabled *Necronomicon*. Unfortunately, the truth is rather less exciting. According to de Camp himself, in a later commentary on the affair, his colleague George Scithers 'decided that if the *Necronomicon* did not exist, it should'. Scithers hired an artist to write a series of squiggles on blank pages to resemble Arabesque calligraphy. De Camp wrote the fanciful introduction, and the book was published in a small print-run of 348 copies, which promptly sold out.

As Lovecraft scholar Dan Clore points out, it would be unfair to describe de Camp and Scithers as hoaxers. Their *Necronomicon* is more a somewhat whimsical 'in-joke', a good-natured jape on those who breathlessly maintain that the book of the mad Arab really exists, and that Lovecraft knew far more than he was letting on when he incorporated it into his stories.

This is exactly the tone taken by the so-called 'Wilson-Hay-Turner-Langford *Necronomicon*', a far more elaborate and substantial affair than the slim de Camp and Scithers offering – although we cannot fairly level the accusation of hoaxing at this volume either. It is more accurate to call it a highbrow spoof.

In his article 'The *Necronomicon*, the Origin of a Spoof', which appeared in the Lovecraft journal *Crypt of Cthulhu*, the world-famous writer on occultism and criminology Colin Wilson describes how George Hay asked him to write an introduction to a volume of stories about the *Necronomicon*. On reading the stories, and finding them undistinguished to say the least, Wilson suggested an altogether more interesting project: to produce the *Necronomicon* itself. Wilson took his inspiration partly from a story by science fiction writer and computer expert David Langford, in which computer analysis of a mysterious manuscript reveals it to be the blasphemous tome. Langford was asked to contribute to the Wilson-Hay project, and provides a detailed and rather complicated section on the methods used to decipher the *Liber Logaeth* manuscript of John Dee. (Langford, incidentally, is the creator of another splendid spoof, the supposed nineteenth-century encounter of an ancestor of his with alien beings – which is still thought genuine by some of the more gullible members of the UFO community.)

The book was published by Neville Spearman in 1978, under the title *The Necronomicon: the Book of Dead Names*, and was reissued in 1992 by the esoteric publisher Skoob Books. For those unfamiliar with Lovecraft and Lovecraft scholarship, the book is immensely misleading, containing as it does many factual errors; however, if one has a little background knowledge of the writer's life and work, it is a hugely enjoyable and entertaining read. In fact, even S. T. Joshi, who takes a very dim view of those who claim that Lovecraft's stories are based on occult 'truths', calls the book 'one of the most exquisite hoaxes of modern times'.

The book begins with a lengthy introduction by Colin Wilson, in which he describes Lovecraft's life, work and personal philosophy. Here, Wilson makes the erroneous claim that Lovecraft's father, Winfield Scott Lovecraft, was a Freemason. It is at this point that one begins to suspect that Wilson has his tongue in his cheek, a suspicion that is confirmed by the inclusion of a letter by a non-existent person called Dr Stanislaus Hinterstoisser. This letter makes the outrageous claim that, through his Masonic contacts, Winfield Lovecraft had been taught to read the *Necronomicon* (which Alessandro Cagliostro had bequeathed to his followers) by a mysterious figure known as 'Tall Cedar'. Wilson amusingly suggests that some of the hallucinations from which Lovecraft's father suffered in his syphilis-induced insanity must have been of the entities he had encountered in the *Necronomicon*.

Of the supposed fragments of the *Necronomicon* included in the volume, there is little to be said beyond Dan Clore's description of them as 'run-of-the-mill occultist fair, with typical magickal recipes utilizing a few Mythos names'. Far more interesting are the three appendices that complete the volume: 'Young Man Lovecraft' by L. Sprague de Camp, 'Dreams of Dead Names: The Scholarship of Sleep' by Christopher Frayling, and 'Lovecraft and Landscape' by Angela Carter.

Clore notes that the material purporting to be from the *Necronomicon* contains a number of inconsistencies with Lovecraft's Mythos. For instance, in Lovecraft's tales the entity Shub-Niggurath, 'the black goat of the woods with a thousand young', is female, whereas in Wilson *et al* it is presented as male. The Great Old Ones are claimed to correspond with the four elements: Air (Hastur), Earth (Shub-Niggurath), Fire (Yog-Sothoth) and Water (Cthulhu). In fact, nowhere in Lovecraft are these or any other entities assigned to the elements: this idea is actually expressed in the stories of Lovecraft's friend and publisher August Derleth, and are inconsistent with Lovecraft's invented universe. Clore also mentions that the spoof *Necronomicon* describes 'the two warring factions, the "Elder Gods" vs the "Great Old Ones", another innovation of Derleth, along with his Christianity-inspired tale of the revolt of the Great Old Ones against their Elders and betters'. He concludes:

> The simple fact is, the vast majority of the material in this version of the *Necronomicon* owes its inspiration not to the Lovecraft Mythos, but to the vastly different Derleth Mythos – when it is not simply supplanted by typical magick recipes.

Unlike the previous two examples, the so-called 'Simon *Necronomicon*' does qualify as a full-blown hoax. The book, published in 1977, is edited by one 'Simon', whose true identity has in itself been the subject of controversy and rumour. One possibility is Herman Slater, proprietor of the Magickal Childe occult bookshop in New York (Clore notes that this establishment is 'mentioned prominently in the volume'). Other possible candidates include L. Sprague de Camp, Colin

Wilson, L. Ron Hubbard (founder of Scientology), the occultist and metaphysical prankster Robert Anton Wilson, and even the Lovecraft-influenced Sandy Pearlman, lyricist for the rock band Blue Oyster Cult.

In his preface, Simon claims to have been given the manuscript by a mysterious priest. Written in Greek, the manuscript bore the title *Necronomicon*, and contained many 'weird drawings'. Simon adds that he was beset with many misfortunes during the book's publication process: a succession of translators was employed (it seems that none suffered the fate of those who worked on the De Camp–Scithers version), the last one making off with his own preface and his translation notes. In addition, Simon himself was 'stricken with a collapsed lung and had to undergo emergency surgery to save his life'.

Clore notes that the majority of the Simon volume is composed of existing translations of Mesopotamian magical texts, with the addition here and there of Lovecraftian names. Most are variations on those to be found in Lovecraft; Cthulhu, for example, becomes Kutulu (such names are usually set in capitals). Simon claims that the name derives from Kutu (the city Kutha) and Lu (man). However, Clore informs us that the proper compound form in Sumerian would be Lu-Kutu. Cthulhu, it should be remembered, is in any case an alien word with no relation whatsoever to any language on Earth and cannot, therefore, be interpreted with reference to human speech.

In conclusion, the 'Simon *Necronomicon*' is a work of demonology that has precious little to do with the Lovecraft Mythos. We must remember that Lovecraft's entities are not gods and demons; they are merely extraterrestrial creatures – albeit immensely intelligent and powerful ones. They do not hate humanity as such; the only reason they would destroy us is because we happen to occupy a planet they consider to be their own. We are like mice in their house: annoying little animals to be swept into oblivion at the first convenient opportunity.

As we have seen, there have been a number of books published over the years claiming to be the long-lost and forbidden *Necronomicon*. Some have been good-natured and well-produced spoofs; while others have been out and out hoaxes. However, there is one book that might just turn out to be the blasphemous tome itself – or at least something very similar. The problem is it is written in a code that, so far, has resisted all attempts at decipherment. It is without doubt the most mysterious book in the world, and occultists have spent decades breathlessly speculating as to the nature of its contents. What strange secrets are written in its pages? Is it the work of some long-dead and unknown wizard, who used the dark arts to gain strange and forbidden knowledge of the Universe? This is certainly implied by the inclusion of drawings that bear a striking resemblance to galaxies, and other drawings of plants that do not exist on Earth. The book is known as the Voynich Manuscript, and the story of its discovery is one of the most intriguing in the history of occultism.

When Wilfred M. Voynich found himself in the library of the Jesuit college at Villa Mondragone in Frascati, near Rome, he could scarcely have guessed at the unique puzzle he was about to discover, a puzzle that remains unsolved to this day. The year was 1912 and Voynich, an unprepossessing antique book dealer and collector, had been accepted by the Jesuits as buyer of part of their manuscript collection, numbering more than 1,000 volumes. The sale was an unfortunate necessity for the college, which needed to fund restorations for the villa. Voynich, who had been introduced to the Jesuits by one Father Strickland S.J., was chosen as buyer over an unnamed Jewish person from Padua, apparently the only other competitor for the right to buy the Mondragone manuscripts.

It is ironic that the serene, tranquil and beautiful countryside of Lazio should have been the location of a discovery that has inspired such frenetic intellectual activity in so many researchers over the years. And yet it was here in the rarefied atmosphere of a theological college that Wilfred Voynich stumbled upon the fantastic enigma that would come to be named after him. Having inspected a number of extremely valuable manuscripts, Voynich picked up a rather drab volume with a limp vellum cover. Although the book was not particularly large (it measured no more than six inches by nine), it was about three inches thick and contained well over 200 pages. The pages were made of soft, light brown calfskin and were uneven at the edges. The volume was held together by three leather thongs and was wrapped in more vellum that had been folded in around the edges to make a cover. When asked about its origin, the priests could only inform Voynich that the book had been discovered in an old chest in the college.

As he carefully leafed through the book, Voynich grew more and more puzzled by its contents. The bizarre illustrations of unknown plants and human figures encased in vessels connected to each other by complex systems of pipes led the collector to suspect that the strange book he held in his hands might hold some profound significance in the history of science. Scanning the text in the not-unreasonable hope that it would reveal something of the book's nature, Voynich was quickly disappointed for it was written exclusively in a beautifully ornate but utterly indecipherable script. The only elements that bore any relation to recognisable reality were the illustrations; and yet even these posed more questions than they answered. What were the strange vessels containing the human figures? Why were they connected to one another by such intricate piping? Were the figures homonculi, artificially created beings; and if so, did this imply some long-lost treatise on alchemy? Perhaps most disturbingly, why did the book contain numerous, carefully drawn illustrations of flowers and plants *that did not exist*?

His curiosity thoroughly piqued, Voynich bought the book, along with thirty or so other manuscripts, from the Jesuits and returned to America, where he immediately began to devote himself to deciphering the mysterious text. He had a number of intriguing clues to guide his investigations, the most important of which were: a letter attached to the book's first page, dated 19 August 1666, by the scientist and Rector of Prague

University, Johannes Marcus Marci, presenting the book to the Jesuit scholar Athanasius Kircher (famous for trying and failing to decipher Egyptian hieroglyphics and for having himself lowered into the crater of Vesuvius to observe the actions of subterranean forces); a faded signature on the first page, indicating that the book had once belonged to one Jacobus de Tepenec; and finally, the fact that the collection housed in the Villa Mondragone had once belonged to the private library of P. Petrus Beckx S.J., 22nd General of the Society of Jesus.

Voynich lost no time in pursuing the first of these clues, the letter from Marci to Kircher, which stated that Marci had received the book from a close friend, and had decided that no one would be able to read it except Kircher. Voynich noted that the book had once belonged to the Holy Roman Emperor Rudolph II of Bohemia, who had paid 600 ducats for it. This was a sizeable amount, equivalent to about $13,000 in Voynich's time. The collector wondered who had presented the book to Rudolph (the letter referred to him only as 'the bearer'), and so he investigated the biographies of many of the known visitors to the Emperor's court. Eventually, he decided that the most promising candidate had to be the famous occultist Dr John Dee. Voynich was convinced that the book itself was the work of Roger Bacon, the English scientist, encyclopaedist, philosopher, alchemist and Franciscan monk, who was known as Doctor Mirabilis (Admirable Doctor) in recognition of his vast range of skills. Dee was a great admirer of Bacon, and was known to have taken a number of the latter's works with him on his European travels.

Voynich decided that the best way to proceed would be to make Photostat copies of the book and circulate them among various scholars whom he assumed would have little trouble deciphering the text. These included palaeographers, medieval historians, cryptographers, linguists, philologists, even astronomers and botanists. Although he had high hopes for a speedy resolution to the enigma, the numerous experts whose help he sought were unable to offer any satisfactory answers.

However, there was plenty of work to be done on the provenance of the book, and Voynich was able to establish that some time after 1608, the manuscript passed to Jacobus de Tepenec, the director of the Emperor's botanical gardens (whose signature was on the first page). When de Tepenec died in 1622, it passed to an unidentified individual, who subsequently left it to Marci in his will. It is not entirely clear what happened to the manuscript between 1666 and 1912, when Voynich acquired it, although it is known that it resided for some time in the private library of Petrus Beckx, who removed it and a number of other manuscripts from the Collegio Romano (now called the Pontificia Università Gregoriana), the main centre of Jesuit learning in Rome, in 1870.

The Pontificia Università Gregoriana is also the repository of the letters received by Athanasius Kircher (a collection known as the *carteggio kircheriano*). Certain material in this collection (not to mention the cryptic letter attached to the manuscript) suggests that the unnamed individual who left the Voynich Manuscript to Johannes Marcus Marci sent several transcribed portions to Kircher; however, there is no record in the *carteggio* of Kircher's response to this material. Intriguingly, there is some evidence that Marci inherited the Voynich Manuscript along with the alchemical library of one George Barschius; and yet he is unknown to historians of alchemy, in spite of there being a letter from him in the *carteggio kircheriano*.

The Voynich Manuscript has become something of a *cause célèbre* in both occult circles and the field of cryptanalysis, by virtue of its utter impenetrability. The cipher in which it is written has defied all attempts at decryption. At first sight, it looks like an ordinary medieval 'herbal', or treatise on the medicinal uses of various plants. This would also explain the astronomical and astrological diagrams. As Colin Wilson reminds us, 'One would expect astronomical or astrological diagrams in a herbal, because the plants were often supposed to be gathered by the full moon, or when the stars or planets were in a certain position.' The only problem is that most of the plants illustrated do not exist. One of the exceptions is a drawing of what looks like a sunflower, which indicates that this part of the book had to have been written after 1492, when Columbus voyaged to America.

The possibility that the manuscript was a hoax perpetrated upon the Emperor Rudolph has prompted researchers to consider having it radiocarbon dated. However, this is unlikely to be of much help, since an accurate dating of the vellum of which the pages are composed would tell us nothing of the date at which the ink was *applied* to those pages.

All of this notwithstanding, Wilfred Voynich had little doubt that the manuscript would yield its secrets once twentieth-century decryption techniques had been applied to it; and so he distributed copies to various interested parties. Unfortunately, the experts who examined the manuscript could not even figure out which language it had been written in prior to encoding. (It could be a natural language, such as English, German, Greek, Hebrew; or an invented language such as the Enochian of John Dee, the *lingua ignota* of Hildegarde von Bingen, Beck's 'Universal Character', or Johnston's 'Synthetic Language'.)

While the secrets of the Voynich Manuscript remain intact, there have been a number of 'false dawns' over the years, notably the work of William Romaine Newbold, a professor of philosophy at the University of Pennsylvania, who in 1921 claimed to have cracked the manuscript's code. According to Newbold, the text had originally been written by Roger Bacon in Latin anagrams, which, once unravelled, revealed that the thirteenth-century philosopher and Franciscan monk possessed an intellect far surpassing that of Galileo or even Isaac Newton. Newbold claimed that the tadpole-like drawings in the manuscript's margins were actually spermatozoa seen under the microscope Bacon had invented. In addition, Bacon had also invented the telescope four centuries before Galileo, through which he had examined the spiral galaxy M31 in Andromeda (at 4.2 million light years, the closest galaxy to our own Milky Way).

In 1931, however, Newbold's conclusions were disproved by the philologist Dr John M. Manly of the University of Chicago, who showed that Newbold's anagramming process could not be counted on to produce accurate results. In addition Newbold had integrated certain unusual manuscript symbols, similar to shorthand, into his interpretative system; but when Manly examined these symbols more closely, he realised that they had been made to look like shorthand by the ink peeling off the vellum in certain places.

The Voynich Manuscript is of interest to cryptanalysts chiefly because of the intriguing intellectual puzzle it presents; while occultists are fascinated by the arcane knowledge it might contain, if only it could be decoded. Indeed, when, in 1960, an antiquarian bookseller named Hans Kraus bought the manuscript from Voynich's widow, Ethel, for no less than $160,000, he suggested that it might well contain astonishing information on the history of humanity. He even maintained that a fair asking price for such information (decoded or not) would be a million dollars. When no one showed any interest in paying this sum, he donated it to Yale University in 1969, where it remains to this day, its secrets intact.

The Voynich Manuscript is one of those fascinating historical puzzles, which, by its very impenetrability, provides us with the perfect template upon which to project our most outlandish fears and desires. For some, it is nothing more than a book on medicinal herbs, a quaint relic of medieval times; while for others the strange diagrams and non-existent plants hint at far stranger information. Some have suggested that, should the Voynich Manuscript ever be deciphered, it will reveal itself to be none other than the frightful *Necronomicon* (Colin Wilson has written a story called 'The Return of the Lloigor' in which this is proved to be the case). If those who suspect this are to be believed, then the day of decipherment will spell the beginning of the end for humanity on Earth.

For, as Lovecraft himself wrote: 'The Old Ones were, the Old Ones are, and the Old Ones shall be again!'

ELEVEN

The Artist

'Resolute imagination is the beginning
of all magical operations.'

PARACELSUS

Few would argue that the process of artistic creation is in many
ways magical, or at least seems so to those who gaze upon the
work of the artist with wonder, appreciation and perhaps a little
jealousy at the application of mysterious skills that would seem
to be for ever beyond his or her reach. Austin Osman Spare was
an artist who gained fame and the breathless admiration of critics at the very outset of his career; yet for him adulation was not
to last, and he ended his days in abject poverty in a grubby basement in South London. His life was as extraordinary as his work,
and perhaps more extraordinary than any artist of the twentieth
century. For not only was Austin Osman Spare a painter and
draughtsman of genius: he was also a wizard, a skilled practitioner of that other art – the art of magic.

Spare was born in Smithfield in 1886, the son of a policeman..
At the age of eighteen, he exhibited at the Royal Academy exhi-
bition of 1904, and had his first West End show at the Bruton
Gallery in 1907. For a short time he attended the Royal College
of Art, but did not complete the course. Although his exhibi-
tions drew great praise from the art establishment (with some
critics comparing his line work with that of Aubrey Beardsley),
others were deeply unsettled by his strange visions. It is said that

George Bernard Shaw considered his work too powerful for normal people.

During the First World War he was conscripted into the Royal Army Medical Corps, and became an official War Artist. Some of his work from this period is preserved in the Imperial War Museum. He edited a journal called *Form – A Quarterly of the Arts*, and was a promoter of automatic drawing long before the idea occurred to the Surrealists. After the war, he edited another artistic journal called *The Golden Hind*, 'a luxury production which became known as "The Golden Behind", due to Spare's fleshy taste in female nudes', according to Phil Baker in his article on Spare in the *Fortean Times*.

There are a number of reasons for Spare's decline into poverty and obscurity, not least of which was his utter disdain for modern art and the people who produced and dealt in it. Allied to this was the fact that he was completely, utterly and proudly working class, and felt far from at ease in the 'polished artistic and literary milieux that he had temporarily moved in'. And so, in the 1920s, he moved back to South London, where he remained for the rest of his life.

As Baker notes, the *fin-de-siècle* was a great time to be interested in magic (not unlike the 1960s, in fact). Although Spare had been too young to join the Hermetic Order of the Golden Dawn, he did join Crowley's breakaway organisation, the Argenteum Astrum in 1909. Although he and Crowley became friends (there may or may not have been a physical element to the relationship), Spare did not remain for long in the organisation, preferring to pursue his own highly individualistic magical agenda.

In his art Spare employed a wide range of styles and mediums, and Baker is right to call it 'exceptionally powerful'. His work has been compared to that of Beardsley, Blake, Dürer and even Michelangelo. Most intriguing from the magical point of view are, of course, his occult drawings, which are expressions of his interest in the nature of belief – as opposed to the question of *what* to believe. Baker compares Crowley's and Spare's attitudes towards magic with Picasso and Marcel Duchamp in the artistic world. He notes that Picasso's position as the greatest artist of the twentieth century has been usurped, according to many, by Marcel Duchamp, whose work comments on the nature of art itself. In a similar way, Spare was more interested in the nature of belief itself than the subjects upon which belief is focused.

When he was seventeen, Spare stayed at the home of the Reverend Robert Hugh Benson, author of several occult novels. While out walking one day, Benson told Spare that he was curious about the young man's magical powers, and wondered whether he would be kind enough to offer a demonstration. It was summer, the weather was particularly fine with not a cloud in the sky. Would Spare be kind enough to produce rain through magical means?

The young artist agreed, and began by drawing a sigil on the back of an old envelope, which he then held before him, focusing his concentration upon it. After about ten minutes, small clouds began to appear in the sky, converging at their position and releasing a downpour that drenched them both.

In his book *The Magical Revival*, Kenneth Grant, Outer Head of the Ordo Templi Orientis and a disciple of Aleister Crowley, describes how Spare had occasion to prove his magical ability again about a year later, when Benson introduced him to Everard Fielding, Secretary of the Society for Psychical Research (SPR). Grant notes that Fielding was acquainted with Frederick Bligh Bond, President of the Archaeological Society, who had discovered the buried Edgar Chapel at Glastonbury Abbey through psychic means. Like Benson, Fielding was intrigued by Spare, and also asked if the young artist might furnish proof of his abilities. Once again, Spare was quite happy to oblige, and asked Fielding what he had in mind. Fielding suggested that he think of an object (which he would not divulge to Spare), and Spare would attempt not only to state the nature of the object, but also to make it materialise out of thin air – in other words, to produce an apport. Spare began by drawing a sigil, which did not represent the unknown object, but rather one of his spirit familiars, to whom he turned for aid whenever mind-reading was required. Presently, Spare received a mental impression of the object in Fielding's mind. He then drew a second sigil, upon which he began to concentrate. At this point, there was a knock at the door. Fielding opened it to find his valet standing there holding Fielding's slippers, which he had indeed chosen to think about.

It was primarily through the use of automatic drawing that Spare performed his magic. He wrote that through the drawing of twisting and interlacing lines, the subconscious mind could express ideas, transferring them (or merely suggesting them) to the consciousness. From these shapes, ideas could be born and developed by the artist. 'By these means, may the profoundest depths of memory be drawn upon and the springs of instinct tapped.' To illustrate his point, Spare notes how Leonardo da Vinci would often derive artistic inspiration from gazing at the random patterns on dirt-streaked walls, or upon the surfaces of striated stones.

According to Spare, handwriting itself is given distinctiveness and expression by an automatic or subconscious nature acquired by habit; and this is also the case with automatic drawing, 'one of the simplest of psychic phenomena', which relies upon the same mental mechanisms that give rise to dreams. Automatic drawing is the 'manifestation of latent desires ... the significance of the forms (the ideas) obtained represent the previous unrecorded obsessions'.

This means of expression thus releases the 'truths' which have been repressed by conventional education, and which lie dormant in the subconscious mind. In effect, the practice of automatic drawing is a magical operation designed to liberate the consciousness and re-establish the practitioner's individuality. Spare warns, however, against the retention of personal biases, convictions and religious beliefs, which can

produce ideas of threat, displeasure or fear, and become obsessions ... In the ecstatic condition of revelation from the subconscious, the mind elevates the sexual or inherited powers (this has no reference to moral theory or practise) and depresses the intellectual qualities. So a new, atavistic responsibility is attained by daring to believe – to possess one's own beliefs – without attempting to rationalize spurious ideas from prejudiced and tainted intellectual sources.

Automatic drawing may be performed either by lengthy concentration upon a sigil, or by any means of pleasantly exhausting both the body and mind, in order to achieve a condition of 'non-consciousness'. One must train oneself to relinquish control over what is being drawn, and to try to draw the entire figure with a single line. 'Drawings should be made by allowing the hand to run freely with the least possible deliberation. In time shapes will be found to evolve, suggesting conceptions, forms and ultimately having personal or individual style.' The mind should be in a state of oblivion, without coherent thought, or the desire to follow whatever is suggested by the conscious intellect; it is only by this means that a condition may be reached in which drawings of 'one's *personal* ideas, symbolic in meaning and wisdom', may be achieved.

There are many tales regarding Spare's skills as a magician, which, as Phil Baker wryly notes, 'make the London Borough of Lambeth seem like H. P. Lovecraft's Arkham County'. One such tale is told by the late scholar Francis X. King, who relates how a young friend of his, an art student, met Spare and got on very well with him. While they agreed that the fashions of modern art were execrable, King's friend could not bring himself to accept the reality of magic. Spare confided in the young man that he was sometimes possessed by the soul of that other great visionary, William Blake, to which his friend responded (perhaps undiplomatically) with a mini-discourse on schizophrenia. This was a little too much for Spare, who told him that he believed wholeheartedly in the reality of magic and the occult, and that, moreover, he had been a practitioner all his life. If his friend wished to see a demonstration, he added, he would be more than happy to oblige the next time they met.

His friend agreed, and a date was set for the demonstration, which would be performed in Spare's dingy basement flat in Brixton. In the intervening days, the younger man had done a little reading on occult subjects, and did not feel quite as confident in his scepticism as he had done at their last meeting. The state of Spare's accommodation did little to help: it was dank, smelly and noisy, with gurgling pipes and buses thundering past outside. Much to the student's surprise, there was none of the dramatic paraphernalia normally associated with practical magic in the room: no crystal balls, no cloaks with embroidered stars and half-moons hanging on the wall, no pointed hats, no wands or magic circles drawn on the floor. There were, however, several sheets of paper containing letters and strange symbols.

When he had finished the piece of pie he was eating, Spare said that the demonstration could begin. He would, he declared, attempt an apportation: the materialisation of a solid object out of thin air. (At that time, apports were still in vogue among Spiritualists.) Spare had decided on a bunch of fresh roses, and began the magical operation by taking up one of the pieces of paper containing the strange symbols and waving it in the air for a few moments. He did this in silence, with a look of fantastically intense concentration on his face, and without any of the incantatory mumbo-jumbo the young art student was expecting. In fact, the only word he uttered, at the end of the operation, was 'Roses'. The two men waited in silence for a few moments, the air in the dingy room thick with expectation of a supernatural event. When the event happened, it was not what either of them was expecting: one of the pipes in the ceiling burst, showering them with an unpleasant mixture of sewage and used bathwater.

As Baker notes, this event was very probably no more than coincidence. However, another tale of Spare's abilities is told by Kenneth Grant. In *The Magical Revival*, Grant relates how Spare was approached by two dabblers in the occult, magical dilettantes who were seeking thrills in the world of the unseen. They asked Spare to conjure up an elemental being, bidding it to take on visible form, their interest having been piqued by their attendance at séances at which they had witnessed materialisations of the dead. In spite of Spare's warning that such entities resided on the atavistic levels of the human subconscious, and thus were potentially extremely dangerous, they begged him to try.

Gradually, a green vapour filled the room and began to coalesce into a man-like figure with glowing eyes and a grinning, idiot face. The entity moved among them, accompanied by an unholy stench. This was more than enough for the two dabblers, who begged Spare to banish the vaporous monstrosity. He quickly complied, and the thing disintegrated before their terrified eyes, leaving an invisible miasma of evil in the room. Grant claims that within weeks one of the dabblers had died of no apparent cause, while the other was committed to an insane asylum.

Although this is a fascinating and spine-tingling story, Baker implies in his article (quite rightly) that it is somewhat redolent of the horror tales of Lovecraft, Arthur Machen and Sax Rohmer (creator of Fu Manchu), whom Grant had enthusiastically read. He goes on to note, however, that late in his life Spare made a curious comment to his friend Frank Letchford. Knowing that Letchford was not interested in the occult, Spare usually steered away from the subject in conversation with him. On this occasion, Spare mentioned that he had become disenchanted with occultism, and that he had had a friend who had delved too deeply and been driven insane.

Equally fascinating (although perhaps just a little less spine-chilling) was an episode that occurred in 1955, one year before Spare's death. At this time, Kenneth Grant was engaged in a magical feud with witchcraft revivalist Gerald Gardner, who believed that Grant had 'poached' one of his mediums, an apparently talented but mentally unstable young woman called Clanda.

Gardner went to see Spare, and asked him for a magical talisman for the restoration of stolen property. He did not provide Spare with any details, and so the artist was unaware that the talisman was to be used in a magical operation directed against

Grant, who was his friend. Spare drew a strange creature, 'a sort of amphibious owl with the wings of a bat and the talons of an eagle', and gave the talisman to Gardner.

Not long after, Grant and Clanda attended a magical meeting at the Islington home of an alchemist. As the ritual began (which apparently was to incarnate the goddess Black Isis), Clanda lay upon an altar, but almost immediately sensed that something was terribly wrong. She claimed later that while on the altar, she felt the temperature in the room drop suddenly, and became aware of a great bird flying into the room. The entity took her up in its great claws and carried her out of the room and the house. She could clearly see the roofs below. Eventually, the bird lost altitude and approached a 'wharf-like structure'. Overcome with terror, Clanda struggled with all her might, and suddenly found herself back on the altar.

Grant later stated that a slimy substance was discovered on the window sill, which – bizarrely – seemed to put forth sprouts or buds.

Spare's thinking on magic is enshrined in three books: *Earth Inferno* (1904), *The Book of Pleasure (Self Love): The Psychology of Ecstasy* (1913) and *The Focus of Life* (1921). His philosophy is based on the central concept of the Kia, which can be described as the state of 'inbetweenness' sometimes equated with the unconscious, combined with another element known as Zos, which represents the human body and mind.

Spare was a fervent believer in reincarnation, and maintained that we retain in our unconscious all the thoughts and experiences of our past lives, whether as humans or animals. He further believed that we can actually observe and communicate with the essences of these previous incarnations or selves, and this was a major inspiration for the strange entities populating his art.

In his magical operations, Spare attempted to pass through these 'levels of being', in the words of Kenneth Grant, to 'penetrate the silent regions of consciously forgotten experiences, evoking by its reverberant power the ineluctable memories that abide perpetually in subconsciousness'. In *The Book of Pleasure*, Spare himself describes his intentions to probe deeply into the subconscious of humanity, which, he believed, contained all the levels of evolutionary being through which humanity had passed to reach its present state. His ultimate goal was to reach what he called the 'Almighty Simplicity', the very essence of life. In so doing, he would gain their properties and power.

Spare believed that this atavistic power could be focused through the use of sigils and other magical formulae composed of words and phrases, which are then either hidden or destroyed, thus banishing their contents into the magician's subconscious mind, where their power can be set to work. It is of the utmost importance not only that the sigil be forgotten, but that the initial desire *itself* also be forgotten. In this way, it can come to dominate the unconscious mind, which nourishes it and increases its power. In *The Magical Revival*, Kenneth Grant explains that conscious desires take time to materialise, while unconscious desires can do so very quickly. In fact, consciousness interferes with the empowerment of the desire.

Spare discovered that the best way to achieve this forgetting, this void within the mind where the initial desire had been, was through physical activity of sufficient intensity as to leave the body exhausted. To achieve this, he employed yogic meditation, which resulted in a trance state in which his body was completely rigid and immobile. He called this 'The Death Posture', and it appears in several of his drawings. Another extremely effective method was Tantric in origin, and involved prolonged masturbation.

As Baker notes, at the time, magical operations involved lengthy preparations using all manner of occult accoutrements and 'often ponderous psychodrama'. Spare would have none of these histrionics, and his own system, in its solitary simplicity, was more akin to the techniques of shamanism than traditional Western occultism, for which he had the utmost contempt.

With his straightforward approach to magic, so very different from that of Crowley (by far the most famous magician of the twentieth century), with its densely written and incredibly complex procedures, it could be argued that Spare's magical legacy is of greater importance to the contemporary scene than Crowley's. The system known as 'Chaos Magic' is the fastest-growing school of modern occultism, and it owes a great deal to Spare's philosophy.

Baker points to another important aspect of Spare's personality: his passion for confabulation. '[A] lie, he used to say, was just a truth in the wrong place.' In 1936, Adolf Hitler offered Spare a commission to paint his portrait; the artist refused, and was briefly lauded in the British press as a result. However, two years later Spare appeared in the papers again when he claimed to have gone to Germany, painted Hitler's portrait, and intended to incorporate it into a magical work against the Nazis. (Exactly how he would have achieved this, since the Führer would probably have wanted to keep his portrait, was never made clear.)

Spare loved to spin a yarn, as can be seen from his assertion that he had studied hieroglyphics in Egypt (plausible), and that he had a letter from Sigmund Freud acknowledging Spare's greater genius (rather less plausible).

Spare himself traced his interest in magic and occultism to the childhood influence of a Mrs Yelga Paterson, an elderly witch who apparently seduced him when he was a youngster. He later claimed that Mrs Paterson had the ability to materialise thought-forms and to tell fortunes with cards. She herself claimed to be descended from a line of Salem witches that Cotton Mather had failed to execute. Spare called her his 'second mother' and, although she was possessed of a rather limited vocabulary, nevertheless she was able to explain the most arcane principles of magic with ease. Although extremely poor, Mrs Paterson would never accept any payment for her fortune-telling, probably because of the widespread belief in occult circles that payment results in the loss of the fortune-telling gift.

When asked to read a person's fortune, Mrs Paterson would occasionally find herself incapable of describing verbally certain future events. On these occasions, she would project the event as a visual image in a dark corner of the room, so that her clients might see for themselves what was in store for them. In *The Magical Revival*, Grant maintains that Spare's interest in the occult was inspired by Mrs Paterson, and was developed with the aid of his great artistic skill.

Mrs Paterson had her own spirit guide, an entity known as Black Eagle, who was the 'control' behind several witch covens, two of which were headed by Mrs Paterson. Black Eagle was apparently of 'Narragansett provenance', and here Grant makes one of his many allusions to the works of H. P. Lovecraft, whom he considers to have been in subconscious contact with the Great Old Ones, or the Outer Ones, the race of godlike extra-terrestrial and extradimensional beings which figure so prominently in the New England fantasist's weird tales.

Following Mrs Paterson's death, Black Eagle 'focused' through Spare, inspiring many of his drawings. One of the covens led by Mrs Paterson was based in a certain region of South Wales, where the witch is said to have invoked Black Eagle 'in the ruins of a twelfth-century edifice in the vicinity of which were found, in 1944, a pair of candlesticks, which, according to informed opinion, are of Florentine workmanship'. These candlesticks were fashioned in the form of a satyr's head. When Grant showed the candlesticks to Spare, he took them to a psychometrist (a psychic who claims the ability to 'read' the history of objects by holding them in his or her hands), who told him that they had belonged to a witch. 'Spare was amused but he did not associate them with Mrs Paterson and the matter was forgotten until 1980, nearly a quarter of a century after his death.' Grant came into contact with an elderly lady who claimed to have been a member of Yelga Paterson's coven around the turn of the twentieth century, and who was able to provide him with information regarding Mrs Paterson's link with the Great Old Ones.

Grant has much more to say on the subject of Spare's connection with the Great Old Ones. For instance, it seems that the name 'Yelga' is actually 'Yelder', an elision of 'Ye Elder'; Grant attributes the mistake to Spare's mild dyslexia, but concedes that the appellation is an appropriate one, since it was through the aged witch that the artist first began his traffic with the occult entities.

According to Grant, there are a number of distinct strands in Spare's work. The influence of Crowley's occult journal *Equinox* (in which Spare published a number of illustrations) is one. Of far greater importance, however, is the influence of the witch Paterson and, through her, that of Black Eagle, 'who transmitted the influence of the Old Ones'. The current of sorcery that flowed from Black Eagle through Mrs Paterson is unthinkably ancient, and it was frequently expressed by Spare in the form of discs and other circular features, which he described as 'Flying Saucers'. This strongly implies a fascinating connection between occultism and ufology, which a number of commentators on the latter subject have suggested over the years. Both Spare and Grant were well aware of this connection.

A detailed discussion of the connections between occultism and ufology is somewhat beyond the scope of this book. However, we may pause briefly to remind ourselves that those connections have formed the basis of some interesting speculations on the true nature of the putative 'visitors from the stars'. Carl Jung, of course, equated the disc shape of many UFOs with the mandala, the circular archetype denoting wholeness and harmony, which, he argued, modern industrial society woefully lacks. This is the prototype of the so-called 'psychosocial hypothesis', which European ufologists have explored (to a far greater extent than their American counterparts).

To Jung, the appearance of discs in the skies, while essentially a psychological phenomenon, nevertheless was a significant expression of human apprehension and uncertainty in the face of the dangers peculiar to modern life (in reference to the Cold War, he said that our world is 'dissociated like a neurotic'). However, Jung stressed that, while his theory suggested a possible *reason* for UFO sightings, it did not explain what UFOs actually *are*.

Indeed, the UFOs' ability to leave physical traces on the ground, and the fact that they are frequently detectable with radar, left Jung as puzzled as any ufologist. At the end of his book *Flying Saucers: A Modern Myth of Things Seen in the Sky*, he admitted the possibility that UFOs are real objects, which afford 'an opportunity for mythological projections'.

Ufologists in the late 1950s, when Jung's book was published, did not welcome his talk of the collective unconscious and psychic materialisations: the general consensus at that time was that UFOs were interplanetary or interstellar spacecraft. It was not until ten years later that a serious ufologist, the French-American astronomer and computer scientist Jacques Vallée, returned to Jung's seminal ideas and expanded them into what would become known as the psychosocial hypothesis. His 1969 book *Passport to Magonia: On UFOs, Folklore and Parallel Worlds* was every bit as radical as Jung's *Flying Saucers* had been a decade earlier. In this book Vallée offered a completely new way of looking at the mystery of UFOs and non-human entities. Comparing the central elements of UFO contacts with those of encounters with supernatural beings in folklore, he suggested that they are manifestations of the same underlying phenomenon, adding that the surface details correspond to the world view prevalent at the time of the encounters. In other words, the fairies, goblins and demons encountered in medieval times (and indeed those entities that occultists have attempted to contact throughout history) have become the alien explorers encountered in recent decades. In later books, such as *Dimensions: A Casebook of Alien Contact* (1988), Vallée suggested that the underlying cause of these multifaceted phenomena may well be an unseen and extremely powerful non-human intelligence, whose intention is to guide the psychic evolution of humanity.

Passport to Magonia proved extremely influential on ufological thinking, prompting other respected researchers, such as Jerome Clark and Loren Coleman, to address the possibilities it raised. In their book *The Unidentified*, Clark and Coleman examined the apparent correlations between ancient and modern encounters uncovered by Vallée, concluding that 'UFO visions are the psyche's attempt to escape the stranglehold that strict rationalism has on modern humanity [and to] restore what is seen as the natural balance between the mind's thinking and feeling aspects'. Ironically, while Clark and Coleman subsequently abandoned these speculations in the face of the physical traces UFOs proved capable of leaving behind, their thoughts nevertheless proved influential in ufology, consolidating the position of the psychosocial hypothesis as a useful tool with which to address the UFO mystery.

It is worth concluding this digression with a few words on the demonic aspect of UFO encounters, where the two fields of ufology and occultism seem to merge in a very unsettling way. As we have noted, the word 'demon' derives from the Greek *daimon*, meaning 'divine power', 'fate' or 'god'. Originally, the word was used to denote spiritual entities intermediate between humans and gods, and as such could be either good or evil. Although rarely alluded to in the literature on UFOs and alien encounters, demonic attributes play a significant part in many reports of human/alien interactions. Those nefarious riders in the night skies, the Greys, are frequently described as demonic, or hideously evil (the American abductee Whitley Strieber originally suspected them of wishing to devour his soul). Indeed, it is interesting to note how the gradual transformation of alien intentions, from the frequently altruistic in the 1950s and 1960s, to the frequently malevolent in the 1980s and 1990s, curiously echoes the transformation of attitudes towards demons, from the 'divine powers' of the Greeks, to the invariably evil entities of the Christian era.

There is an additional parallel to be found in the preoccupation with human sexuality evinced by both demons and aliens. The former were very fond of tormenting their human victims sexually (men being seduced by succubi, women by incubi); the latter are obsessed with impregnating human females and extracting the sperm of human males, some of whom have related appalling tales of being physically seduced by female

Greys. The often-reported scars and 'scoop marks' (indentations in the skin, where tissue has apparently been removed) on the bodies of abductees likewise seem comparable to the skin blemishes by which medieval witches could allegedly be detected.

Later, in *Outer Gateways* (1994), Grant paused to consider the occult meaning of the Lovecraft Mythos. (It should not be forgotten that Lovecraft, who invented these entities, had nothing but contempt for professional occultists like Grant. Indelicate as the metaphor is, the gentleman of Providence must be spinning in his grave at the thought that so many occultists believe he was in unwitting contact with these entities – or entities very much like them – which provided him via his frequent nightmares with material for his strange tales.)

The Lovecraft Mythos, Grant maintains, reflects 'vastly ancient pre-human lore', an unclassifiable phase of our planet's history. The entities themselves are representative of the subconscious and the cosmic forces existing beyond our narrow awareness, and true creativity occurs only when these forces are invoked 'to flood with their light the magical network of the mind'.

Grant envisages the mind as divided into three rooms, or compartments: the subconscious, or dream state; the mundane consciousness, or waking state; and the transcendental consciousness. Through a system of 'conduits or tunnels', these rooms are connected with the house that contains them; the house itself represents 'trans-terrestrial consciousness'. In the magical universe of Grant and Spare, the forces from 'Outside' (the Great Old Ones) are not seen as evil or destructive, but rather as dynamic and liberating energies 'the functions of which are to blast away the delusion of separate existence (the rooms of our illustration)'. For this reason, the magician must remember that danger is not inherent in the Great Old Ones themselves, but rather in the attitude he or she adopts towards them when performing magical operations.

In one form or another, the Great Old Ones appear in the myths of humanity throughout history. However, Grant maintains that it was Lovecraft himself who 'traced in his tales of the

Cthulhu Myth Cycle the most significant map of the pre-human Gnosis'. As we have noted, Lovecraft was a great dreamer, and some of his strangest and most unsettling tales seem to have been transcribed more or less directly from his own fantastic nightmares. The Great Old Ones are said to communicate with humanity through dreams, the most profound contact being reserved for those 'peculiarly fitted to respond to Their vibrations'. Fortunately or unfortunately, Lovecraft himself was one of these people, exemplifying Grant's contention that many dreamers who attempt to establish contact with the outer entities fail to do so, while others, who (like Lovecraft) have little or no interest in such bizarre traffic, succeed spectacularly.

As we have seen, there is a strong thematic thread running from Lovecraft's work to Austin Spare's. The power of their imaginations and the nature of the material they produced make them kindred spirits; however, they differed fundamentally in their attitudes to that material. While Lovecraft considered himself a writer of weird fiction and no more, Spare believed unequivocally in the power of his own art to place him in contact with the potent denizens of the outer realms of space and time.

Conclusion

The world of the wizard is a far larger and more complex realm than one might gather from the traditional image of the bearded worker of magic in the pointed hat. We have seen how he was present at the dawn of civilisation, a mysterious intermediary between the world of mortals and the vast and unknown territory of the supernatural surrounding our tiny island of humanity. Shamanic cultures looked to their holy men for healing and guidance, as did the first great civilisations of Mesopotamia, whose own wizards formed the first links in an occult chain stretching throughout history to the present day.

They wandered through the ancient world, dispensing wisdom to some and bringing the wrath of unknown realms upon others; feared and hated by many, they were respected by all. In accordance with the fundamental guiding principle of magic, the wizards attempted to gain mastery over reality itself through an understanding of the fundamental forces of nature. We have seen that this thirst for knowledge has been common to all times, and that the alchemist using the principles of magic to transform base metals into gold was not so very different from the modern chemist attempting to learn the secrets of the molecular world. Many of the goals towards which the wizards worked are goals many of us would like to attain today: for some religious people, Spiritualism is but a version of necromancy, and is equally dangerous.

This book has been an attempt to acquaint the reader with the lives and adventures of some of the more colourful characters that have strode across the dark stage of the occult over the centuries. Some, as in the case of H. P. Lovecraft, have had an enormous influence on modern practitioners of the magical arts; and while many would say that he was not a wizard, others would claim that this is precisely what he was (although he himself was unaware of the fact). Kenneth Grant, a magician of considerable standing, certainly held this view, maintaining in his many books that Lovecraft was in intimate – if unwitting – contact with extremely powerful and potentially dangerous occult forces, which found their full expression in his sinister and wonderful stories. In other words, Lovecraft was, in effect, a living conduit between this world and the vast and terrible mysteries of other worlds and dimensions, which is one definition of a wizard.

In the final analysis, of course, it is up to the reader to decide whether magicians such as John Dee, Aleister Crowley, Jack Parsons and Austin Osman Spare were really in touch with influences and intelligences beyond the sphere in which we conduct our day-to-day lives. Do we have anything to fear from them and people like them, whose curiosity about the Universe compels them to reach with their minds into realms perhaps best left alone? It is difficult to say with any certainty. Without doubt, some magical experiments can have serious consequences for those brave or foolish enough to attempt them. As for the rest of us, we can only read with fascination of their exploits in the worlds of the occult, and hope we are never made to pay the price for the wizard's knowledge.

Bibliography and suggested further reading

BOOKS AND ARTICLES

Anderson, Ken: *Hitler and the Occult*. Amherst, New York, Prometheus Books, 1995.

Baigent, Michael and Leigh, Richard: *The Elixir and the Stone: The Tradition of Magic and Alchemy*. London, Viking, 1997.

Baker, Alan: *Invisible Eagle: The History of Nazi Occultism*. London, Virgin Publishing, 2000.

Baker, Phil: 'Stroke of Genius'. Profile of Austin Osman Spare in *Fortean Times* 144.

Bennett, Colin: 'Rocket in his Pocket'. Profile of Jack Parsons in *Fortean Times* 132.

Brandreth, Gyles: 'An Interview with Father Gabriele Amorth, the Church's Leading Exorcist'. *Sunday Telegraph* (London), 29 October 2000.

Cannon, Peter (Ed): *Lovecraft Remembered*. Sauk City, Wisconsin, Arkham House Publishers, 1998.

Carter, John: *Sex and Rockets: The Occult World of Jack Parsons*. Venice, California, Feral House, 1999.

Cavendish, Richard: *The Magical Arts*. London, Arkana, 1984.

Chapman, Douglas: 'Jack Parsons: Sorcerous Scientist'. *Strange Magazine* No. 6.

Crowley, Aleister: *Magick*. London, RKP, 1973.

Daraul, Arkon: *A History of Secret Societies*. New York, Citadel Press, 1994.

David-Neel, Alexandra: *With Mystics and Magicians in Tibet.* London, Lane, 1934.

_____: *Magic and Mystery in Tibet.* New York, Crown, 1937.

Drury, Nevill: *The Elements of Shamanism.* Shaftsbury, Dorset, Element Books, 1989.

Fest, Joachim C.: *Hitler.* London, Penguin Books, 1974.

Grant, Kenneth: *Outer Gateways.* London, Skoob Books Publishing, 1994.

_____: *Cults of the Shadow.* London, Muller, 1975.

_____: *The Magical Revival.* London, Muller, 1972.

_____: *Outside the Circles of Time.* London, Muller, 1980.

Guiley, Rosemary Ellen: *Harper's Encyclopedia of Mystical & Paranormal Experience.* New Jersey, Castle Books, 1991.

Hay, George (Ed): *The Necronomicon: The Book of Dead Names.* London, Skoob Books Publishing, 1992.

Joshi, S. T.: *A Subtler Magick: The Writings and Philosophy of H. P. Lovecraft.* San Bernardino, California, The Borgo Press, 1982.

Le Page, Victoria: *Shambhala: The Fascinating Truth Behind the Myth of Shangri-la.* Wheaton, Illinois, Quest Books, 1996.

Lévy, Maurice: *Lovecraft: A Study in the Fantastic.* Detroit, Michigan, Wayne State University Press, 1988.

Lovecraft, H. P.: *The Annotated H. P. Lovecraft* (ed. S. T. Joshi). New York, Dell Publishing, 1997.

Neihardt, John G.: *Black Elk Speaks.* Online version.

Pauwels, Louis and Bergier, Jacques: *The Morning of the Magicians.* London, Mayflower Books, 1971.

Poncé, Charles: *Kabbalah.* Wheaton, Illinois, Quest Books, 1995.

Roerich, Nicholas: *Shambhala.* New York, Nicholas Roerich Museum, 1978.

Russell, Jeffrey B.: *A History of Witchcraft: Sorcerers, Heretics and Pagans.* London, Thames and Hudson, 1991.

Simon: *The Necronomicon.* New York, Avon Books, 1977.

Spare, Austin Osman: *The Book of Pleasure.* Montréal, 93 Publishing, 1975.

Spence, Lewis: *An Encyclopedia of Occultism*. New York, Carol Publishing Group, 1996.

Summers, Montague: *History of Witchcraft and Demonology*. New York, Knopf, 1926.

Symonds, John: *The Magic of Aleister Crowley*. London, Muller, 1958.

Thomas, Keith: *Religion and the Decline of Magic*. London, Weidenfeld & Nicolson, 1971.

Tomas, Andrew: *Shambhala: Oasis of Light*. London, Sphere Books, 1977.

Underwood, Peter: *Dictionary of the Supernatural*. London, Harrap, 1978.

Webb, James: *The Occult Underground*. La Salle, Illinois, Open Court Publishing, 1974.

Wedeck, Harry E. (Ed): *A Treasury of Witchcraft: A Sourcebook of the Magic Arts*. New York, Gramercy Books, 1961.

Wilson, Robert Anton: *Cosmic Trigger: Final Secret of the Illuminati*. Phoenix, Arizona, New Falcon Publications, 1993.

WEBSITES

The Youth of Apollonius at http://www.alchemylab.com
Great Theosophists at http://www.wisdomworld.org
The New Advent Catholic Encyclopedia
  at http://www.newadvent.org/cathen
Encyclopedia.com at http://www.encyclopedia.com

Index